Exercises to Accompany

THE

LITTLE,

BROWN

COMPACT

HANDBOOK

SIXTH EDITION

Jane E. Aaron

PEARSON
Longman

New York   Boston   San Francisco
London   Toronto   Sydney   Tokyo   Singapore   Madrid
Mexico City   Munich   Paris   Cape Town   Hong Kong   Montreal

Acquisitions Editor: Brandon Hight
Senior Supplements Editor: Donna Campion
Development Editor: Carol M. Hollar-Zwick
Electronic Page Makeup: Dianne Hall

Exercises to Accompany The Little, Brown Compact Handbook,
Sixth Edition

ISBN: 0-321-42885-4

2 3 4 5 6 7 8 9 10–CRW–09 08

PREFACE

The exercises in this book give students a chance to try out what they have learned from *The Little, Brown Compact Handbook*, Sixth Edition. The exercises range from revising paragraphs through correcting grammar and punctuation to paraphrasing sources and writing works-cited entries. With a few exceptions, the work can be completed on the pages of this book. Like actual writing, the exercises are in connected discourse, with sentences building passages on cross-disciplinary topics such as literature, business practice, and animal behavior.

Each exercise is keyed to the relevant chapter and section(s) in *The Little, Brown Compact Handbook*, or LBCH for short, as in this sample exercise heading:

Exercise 15.1   *LBCH 15a*
Revising: Emphasis of subjects and verbs

Students who have difficulty with any exercise should read the appropriate text explanation and then try again.

Some exercises include an example illustrating what is required to complete the exercise. For nearly all the exercises, one or more sample answers appear at the back of this book. These features assist instructors in discussing exercises with students and help those students working independently. These samples and the rest of the answers for each exercise appear in a separate answer key, which instructors may reproduce for distribution to students.

Answers are labeled "possible" when the corresponding exercises encourage choice in responding and the given answers are but suggestions. Even for the objective exercises, which more often lend themselves to one response, some users may disagree with some answers. Usage is often flexible, and many rules allow interpretation. The answers here conform to the usage recommended in *The Little, Brown Compact Handbook*.

CONTENTS

1
THE WRITING PROCESS

2
WRITING IN AND OUT OF COLLEGE

3
CLARITY AND STYLE

4

SENTENCE PARTS AND PATTERNS

Basic Grammar

Verbs

Pronouns

Modifiers

5

PUNCTUATION

6

SPELLING AND MECHANICS

7

RESEARCH WRITING

8

WRITING IN THE DISCIPLINES

PART 1

The Writing Process

Exercise 3.1 Evaluating thesis statements   LBCH 3a

Evaluate the following thesis statements, considering whether each one is sufficiently limited, specific, and unified. Rewrite the statements as necessary to meet these goals.

*1 Aggression usually leads to violence, injury, and even death, and we should use it constructively.

*2 The religion of Islam is widely misunderstood in the United States.

3 One evening of a radio talk show amply illustrates both the appeal of such shows and their silliness.

4 Good manners make our society work.

5 The poem is about motherhood.

*Sample answer provided at the back of the book.

6 Television is useful for children and a mindless escape for adults who do not want to think about their problems.

7 I disliked American history in high school, but I like it in college.

8 Drunken drivers, whose perception and coordination are impaired, should receive mandatory suspensions of their licenses.

9 Business is a good major for many students.

10 The state's lenient divorce laws undermine the institution of marriage, which is fundamental to our culture, and they should certainly be made stricter for couples who have children.

Exercise 3.2 Organizing ideas   LBCH 3b

The following list of ideas was extracted by a student from freewriting he did for a brief paper on soccer in the United States. Using his thesis statement as a guide, pick out the general ideas and arrange the relevant specific points under them. In some cases you may have to infer general ideas to cover specific points in the list. (A partial sample outline appears at the end of the book.)

Thesis statement

Soccer will probably never be the sport in the United States that it is elsewhere because both the potential fans and the potential backers resist it.

List of ideas

Sports seasons are already too crowded for fans.

Soccer rules are confusing to Americans.

A lot of kids play soccer in school, but the game is still "foreign."

Sports money goes where the money is.

Backers are wary of losing money on new ventures.

Fans have limited time to watch.

Fans have limited money to pay for sports.

Backers are concerned with TV contracts.

Previous attempts to start a pro soccer league failed.

TV contracts almost matter more than live audiences.

Failure of the US Football League was costly.

Baseball, football, hockey, and basketball seasons overlap.

Soccer fans couldn't fill huge stadiums.

American soccer fans are too few for TV interest.

PART 2

Writing in and out of College

Exercise 8.1 Using academic language   LBCH 8e

Revise the following paragraph to make the language more academic while keeping the factual information the same.

*If you buy into the stereotype of girls chatting away on their cell phones, you should think again. One of the major wireless companies surveyed 1021 cell phone owners for a period of five years and—surprise!—reported that guys talk on cell phones more than girls do. In fact, guys were way ahead of girls, using an average of 571 minutes a month compared to 424 for girls. That's 35 percent more time on the phone! The survey also asked about conversations on home phones, and while girls still beat the field, the guys are catching up.

*Sample answer provided at the back of the book.

Exercise 11.1   *LBCH 11a*
Testing argument subjects

Analyze each subject below to determine whether it is appropriate for argument. Explain your reasoning in each case.

*1 Granting of athletic scholarships

*2 Care of automobile tires

3 Censoring the Web sites of hate groups

4 History of the town park

5 Housing for the homeless

6 Billboards in urban residential areas or in rural areas

7 Animal testing for cosmetics research

*Sample answer provided at the back of the book.

8 Cats versus dogs as pets

9 Ten steps in recycling wastepaper

10 Benefits of being a parent

Exercise 11.2   *LBCH 11b*
Identifying and revising fallacies

Fallacies tend to appear together, as each of the following sentences illustrates. Identify at least one fallacy in each sentence. Then revise the sentences to make them more reasonable.

*1 The American government can sell nuclear technology to non-nuclear nations, so why can't individuals, who after all have a God-given right to earn a living as they see fit?

2 A successful marriage demands a maturity that no one under twenty-five possesses.

3 Students' persistent complaints about the grading system prove that it is unfair.

*Sample answer provided at the back of the book.

4 People watch television because they are too lazy to talk or read or because they want mindless escape from their lives.

5 Racial tension is bound to occur when people with different back-grounds are forced to live side by side.

PART 3

Clarity and Style

Exercise 15.1   *LBCH 15a*
Revising: Emphasis of subjects and verbs

Rewrite the sentences in the following paragraph so that their subjects and verbs identify the key actors and actions.

*1 Many heroes were helpful in the emancipation of the slaves. *2 However, the work of Harriet Tubman, an escaped slave herself, stands above the rest. 3 Tubman's accomplishments included the guidance of hundreds of slaves to freedom on the Underground Railroad. 4 A return to slavery was risked by Tubman or possibly death. 5 During the Civil War she was also a carrier of information from the South to the North. 6 After the war Tubman was instrumental in helping to raise money for former slaves who were in need of support.

*Sample answer provided at the back of the book.

Exercise 15.2   LBCH 15b
Sentence combining: Beginnings and endings

Locate the main idea in each group of sentences below. Then combine each group into a single sentence that emphasizes that idea by placing it at the beginning or the end. For sentences 2–5, determine the position of the main idea by considering its relation to the previous sentences: if the main idea picks up a topic that's already been introduced, place it at the beginning; if it adds new information, place it at the end.

Example:
The storm blew roofs off buildings. It caused extensive damage. It knocked down many trees.

Main idea at beginning: <u>The storm caused extensive damage,</u> blowing roofs off buildings and knocking down many trees.

Main idea at end: Blowing roofs off buildings and knocking down many trees, <u>the storm caused extensive damage.</u>

*1 Pat Taylor strode into the room. The room was packed. He greeted students called "Taylor's Kids." He nodded to their parents and teachers.

*2 This was a wealthy Louisiana oilman. He had promised his "Kids" free college educations. He was determined to make higher education available to all qualified but disadvantaged students.

3 The students welcomed Taylor. Their voices joined in singing. They sang "You Are the Wind Beneath My Wings." Their faces beamed with hope. Their eyes flashed with self-confidence.

*Sample answer provided at the back of the book.

4 The students had thought a college education was beyond their dreams. It seemed too costly. It seemed too demanding.

5 Taylor had to ease the costs and the demands of getting to college. He created a bold plan. The plan consisted of scholarships, tutoring, and counseling.

Exercise 15.3   *LBCH 15c*
Sentence combining: Coordination

Combine sentences in the following passages to coordinate related ideas in the ways that seem most effective to you. You will have to supply coordinating conjunctions or conjunctive adverbs and the appropriate punctuation.

1 Many chronic misspellers do not have the time to master spelling rules. They may not have the motivation. They may rely on dictionaries to catch misspellings. Most dictionaries list words under their correct spellings. One kind of dictionary is designed for chronic misspellers. It lists each word under its common *mis*spellings. It then provides the correct spelling. It also provides the definition.

*Sample answer provided at the back of the book.

2 Henry Hudson was an English explorer. He captained ships for the
   Dutch East India Company. On a voyage in 1610 he passed by
   Greenland. He sailed into a great bay in today's northern Canada.
   He thought he and his sailors could winter there. The cold was terrible. Food ran out. The sailors mutinied. The sailors cast Hudson
   adrift in a small boat. Eight others were also in the boat. Hudson
   and his companions perished.

Exercise 15.4   *LBCH 15d*
Revising: Subordination for emphasis

Emphasize the important information in the following paragraph
by giving it in main clauses and subordinating other information.

*1 During the Civil War, soldiers often admired their commanding

officers, and they gave them nicknames, and these names frequently

contained the word *old*, but not all of the commanders were old. *2

Confederate General Thomas "Stonewall" Jackson was also called

"Old Jack," and he was not yet forty years old. 3 Another Southern

general in the Civil War was called "Old Pete," and his full name was

*Sample answer provided at the back of the book.

James Longstreet. **4** The Union general Henry W. Halleck had a reputation as a good military strategist, and he was an expert on the work of a French military authority, Henri Jomini, and Halleck was called "Old Brains." **5** Well before the Civil War, General William Henry Harrison won the Battle of Tippecanoe, and he received the nickname "Old Tippecanoe," and he used the name in his presidential campaign slogan, "Tippecanoe and Tyler, Too," and he won the election in 1840, but he died of pneumonia a month after taking office.

Exercise 15.5   *LBCH 15d*
Sentence combining: Subordination

Combine each of the following pairs of sentences twice, each time using one of the subordinate structures in parentheses to make a single sentence. You will have to add, delete, change, and rearrange words.

> *Example:*
>
> During the late eighteenth century, workers carried beverages in brightly colored bottles. The bottles had cork stoppers. (*Clause beginning <u>that</u>. Phrase beginning <u>with</u>.*)
>
> During the late eighteenth century, workers carried beverages in brightly colored bottles <u>that had cork stoppers</u>.
>
> During the late eighteenth century, workers carried beverages in brightly colored bottles <u>with cork stoppers</u>.

*1 The bombardier beetle sees an enemy. It shoots out a jet of chemicals to protect itself. (*Clause beginning* <u>when</u>. *Phrase beginning* <u>seeing</u>.)

2 The beetle's spray is very potent. It consists of hot and irritating chemicals. (*Phrase beginning* <u>consisting</u>. *Phrase beginning* <u>of</u>.)

3 The spray's two chemicals are stored separately in the beetle's body and mixed in the spraying gland. The chemicals resemble a nerve-gas weapon. (*Phrase beginning* <u>stored</u>. *Clause beginning* <u>which</u>.)

4 The tip of the beetle's abdomen sprays the chemicals. The tip revolves like a turret on a World War II bomber. (*Phrase beginning* <u>revolving</u>. *Phrase beginning* <u>spraying</u>.)

5 The beetle defeats most of its enemies. It is still eaten by spiders and birds. (*Clause beginning* <u>although</u>. *Phrase beginning* <u>except</u>.)

Exercise 15.6   *LBCH 15d*
Revising: Effective subordination

Revise the following paragraph to eliminate faulty or excessive subordination and thus to emphasize the main ideas. Correct faulty subordination by reversing main and subordinate structures. Correct excessive subordination by coordinating equal ideas or by making separate sentences.

*Sample answer provided at the back of the book.

*1 Genaro González is a successful writer, which means that his stories and novels have been published to critical acclaim. 2 In interviews, he talks about his love of writing, even though he has also earned a doctorate in psychology because he enjoys teaching. 3 González's first story, which reflects his growing consciousness of his Aztec heritage and place in the world, is titled "Un Hijo del Sol." 4 He wrote the first version of "Un Hijo del Sol" while he was a sophomore at the University of Texas-Pan American, which is in the Rio Grande valley of southern Texas, which González called "el Valle" in the story, and where he now teaches psychology. 5 González, who writes equally well in English and Spanish, received a large fellowship that enabled him to take a leave of absence from his teaching job at Pan American so that for a year he could write full-time.

Exercise 15.7   LBCH 15c, 15d
Revising: Coordination and subordination

The following paragraph consists entirely of simple sentences. Use coordination and subordination to combine sentences in the ways you think most effective to emphasize main ideas.

*Sample answer provided at the back of the book.

*Sir Walter Raleigh personified the Elizabethan Age. *That was the period of Elizabeth I's rule of England. *The period occurred in the last half of the sixteenth century. Raleigh was a courtier and poet. He was also an explorer and entrepreneur. Supposedly, he gained Queen Elizabeth's favor. He did this by throwing his cloak beneath her feet at the right moment. She was just about to step over a puddle. There is no evidence for this story. It does illustrate Raleigh's dramatic and dynamic personality. His energy drew others to him. He was one of Elizabeth's favorites. She supported him. She also dispensed favors to him. However, he lost his queen's goodwill. Without her permission he seduced one of her maids of honor. He eventually married the maid of honor. Elizabeth died. Then her successor imprisoned Raleigh in the Tower of London. Her successor was James I. The king falsely charged Raleigh with treason. Raleigh was released after thirteen years. He was arrested again two years later on the old treason charges. At the age of sixty-six he was beheaded.

*Sample answer provided at the back of the book.

Exercise 16.1 Revising: Parallelism   LBCH 16

Revise the following paragraph as needed to create parallelism for grammar and coherence. Add or delete words or rephrase as necessary.

*1 The ancient Greeks celebrated four athletic contests: the Olympic Games at Olympia, the Isthmian Games were held near Corinth, at Delphi the Pythian Games, and the Nemean Games were sponsored by the people of Cleonae. **2** Each day the games consisted of either athletic events or holding ceremonies and sacrifices to the gods. **3** Competitors participated in running sprints, spectacular chariot and horse races, and running long distances while wearing full armor. **4** The purpose of such events was developing physical strength, demonstrating skill and endurance, and sharpening the skills needed for war. **5** The athletes competed less to achieve great wealth than for gaining honor both for themselves and their cities. **6** Of course, exceptional athletes received financial support from patrons, poems and statues by admiring artists, and they even got lavish living quarters

*Sample answer provided at the back of the book.

from their sponsoring cities. **7** With the medal counts and flag cere-

monies, today's Olympians sometimes seem to be proving their coun-

tries' superiority more than to demonstrate individual talent.

Exercise 16.2   **LBCH 16**
Sentence combining: Parallelism

Combine each group of sentences below into one concise sentence
in which parallel elements appear in parallel structures. You will
have to add, delete, change, and rearrange words. Each item has
more than one possible answer.

Example:
The new process works smoothly. It is efficient, too.
The new process works smoothly and <u>efficiently</u>.

*1 People can develop post-traumatic stress disorder (PTSD). They
develop it after experiencing a dangerous situation. They will also
have felt fear for their survival.

2 The disorder can be triggered by a wide variety of events. Combat
is a typical cause. Similarly, natural disasters can result in PTSD.
Some people experience PTSD after a hostage situation.

3 PTSD can occur immediately after the stressful incident. Or it may
not appear until many years later.

*Sample answer provided at the back of the book.

4 Sometimes people with PTSD will act irrationally. Moreover, they often become angry.

5 Other symptoms include dreaming that one is reliving the experience. They include hallucinating that one is back in the terrifying place. In another symptom one imagines that strangers are actually one's former torturers.

Exercise 17.1 Revising: Variety   LBCH 17

The following paragraph consists entirely of simple sentences that begin with their subjects. Use the techniques discussed in this chapter to vary the sentences. Delete, add, change, and rearrange words to make the paragraph more readable and to make important ideas stand out clearly.

*The Italian volcano Vesuvius had been dormant for many years.

*It then exploded on August 24 in the year AD 79. The ash, pumice, and mud from the volcano buried two busy towns. Herculaneum is one. The more famous is Pompeii. Both towns lay undiscovered for many centuries. Herculaneum and Pompeii were discovered in 1709 and 1748, respectively. The excavation of Pompeii was the more systematic. It was the occasion for initiating modern methods of conser-

*Sample answer provided at the back of the book.

vation and restoration. Herculaneum was simply looted of its more valuable finds. It was then left to disintegrate. Pompeii appears much as it did before the eruption. A luxurious house opens onto a lush central garden. An election poster decorates a wall. A dining table is set for breakfast.

Exercise 18.1   LBCH 18a
Revising: Appropriate words

Rewrite the following paragraphs as needed for standard American English, focusing on inappropriate slang, technical or pretentious language, and biased language. Consult a dictionary to determine whether particular words are appropriate and to find suitable substitutes.

*1 Acquired immune deficiency syndrome (AIDS) is a major deal all over the world, and those who think the disease is limited to homos, druggies, and foreigners are quite mistaken. *2 Indeed, stats suggest that in the United States one in every five hundred American college kids carries the HIV virus that causes AIDS. *3 If such numbers are to be believed, then doctors and public health officials will con-

*Sample answer provided at the back of the book.

tinue to have a whole lot of HIV and AIDS victims on their hands in the years to come.

4 A person with HIV or a full-blown AIDS sufferer deserves to be treated with respect, like someone with any other disease. **5** He should not be dissed or subjected to exclusionary behavior on the part of his fellow citizens. **6** Instead, each victim has the necessity for all the medical care and financial assistance due those who are in the extremity of illness. **7** Many professionals in the medical and social services communities are committed to helping HIV and AIDS patients. **8** For example, a doctor may help his patients by obtaining social services for them as well as by providing medical care. **9** A social worker may visit an HIV or AIDS victim and determine whether he qualifies for public assistance, since many patients don't have the dough for insurance or drugs. **10** Patients who are very ill may require the ministrations of a home-care nurse. **11** She can administer medications and make the sick person as comfy as possible.

Exercise 18.2
Revising: Sexist language

Revise the following paragraph to eliminate sexist language. If you change a singular noun or pronoun to plural, be sure to make any needed changes in verbs or other pronouns.

*1 When a student applies for a job, he should prepare the best possible résumé, because the businessman who is scanning a stack of résumés will read them all quickly. *2 The person who wants his résumé to stand out will make sure it highlights his best points. 3 A person applying for a job as a mailman should emphasize his honesty and responsibility. 4 A girl applying for a position as a home-care nurse should also emphasize her honesty and responsibility as well as her background of capable nursing. 5 Someone seeking work as a computer programmer will highlight his experience with computers. 6 Students without extensive job experience should highlight their volunteer work. 7 For instance, a student may have been chairman of a campus organization or secretary of her church's youth group. 8 If everyone writing a résumé considers what the man who will read it is

*Sample answer provided at the back of the book.

looking for, the applicant will know better what he should include and

how he should format that information.

Exercise 18.3 Using a dictionary   *LBCH 18b*

Look up five of the following words in a dictionary. For each word, write down (a) the division into syllables, (b) the pronunciation, (c) the grammatical functions and forms, (d) the etymology, (e) each meaning, and (f) any special uses indicated by labels. Finally, use the word in two sentences of your own.

1 depreciation

2 secretary

3 grammar

4 manifest

5 assassin

6 astrology

7 toxic

8 steal

9 plain (*adjective*)

10 ceremony

Exercise 18.4 Revising: Denotation   LBCH 18b

Revise any underlined word below that is used incorrectly. Consult a dictionary if you are uncertain of a word's precise meaning.

*1 The acclaimed writer Maxine Hong Kingston <u>sites</u> her mother's stories about ancestors and ancient Chinese customs as the sources of her first two books, *The Woman Warrior* and *China Men*. 2 One of her mother's tales, about a pregnant aunt who was <u>ostracized</u> by villagers, had a great <u>affect</u> on the young Kingston. 3 The aunt gained <u>avengeance</u> by drowning herself in the village water supply. 4 Kingston made the aunt <u>infamous</u> by giving her <u>immortality</u> in *The Woman Warrior*. 5 Two of Kingston's <u>progeny</u>, her great-grandfathers, are the focal points of *China Men*. 6 Both men led rebellions against <u>suppressive</u> employers: a sugar-cane farmer and a railroad-construction engineer. 7 Kingston's innovative writing <u>infers</u> her opposition to racism and sexism both in the China of the past and in the United States of the present. 8 She was <u>rewarded</u> many prizes for these distinguished books.

*Sample answer provided at the back of the book.

Exercise 18.5   *LBCH 18b*
Considering the connotation of words

Fill in the blank in each sentence below with the most appropriate word from the list in parentheses. Consult a dictionary to be sure of your choice.

*1 Infection with the AIDS virus, HIV, is a serious health _____.
    (*problem, worry, difficulty, plight*)

2 Once the virus has entered the blood system, it _____ T-cells.
    (*murders, destroys, slaughters, executes*)

3 The _____ of T-cells is to combat infections. (*ambition, function, aim, goal*)

4 Without enough T-cells, the body is nearly _____ against infections. (*defenseless, hopeless, desperate*)

5 To prevent exposure to the virus, one should be especially _____ in sexual relationships. (*chary, circumspect, cautious, calculating*)

*Sample answer provided at the back of the book.

Exercise 18.6   LBCH 18b
Revising: Concrete and specific words

Make the following paragraph vivid by expanding the sentences with appropriate details of your own choosing. Substitute concrete and specific words for the abstract and general ones that are underlined.

*1 I remember clearly how awful I felt the first time I attended Mrs.

Murphy's second-grade class. **2** I had recently moved from a small

town in Missouri to a crowded suburb of Chicago. **3** My new school

looked big from the outside and seemed dark inside as I walked down

the long corridor toward the classroom. **4** The class was noisy as I

neared the door; but when I entered, everyone became quiet and

looked at me. **5** I felt uncomfortable and wanted a place to hide.

6 However, in a loud voice Mrs. Murphy directed me to the front of the

room to introduce myself.

Exercise 18.7   LBCH 18b
Using concrete and specific words

For each abstract or general word below, give at least two other words or phrases that are increasingly specific or concrete. Consult a dictionary as needed. Use the most specific or concrete word from each group in a sentence of your own.

*Sample answer provided at the back of the book.

Example:
awake, <u>watchful</u>, <u>vigilant</u>
<u>Vigilant</u> guards patrol the buildings.

*1 fabric

*2 delicious

3 car

4 narrow-minded

5 reach (*verb*)

6 green

*Sample answer provided at the back of the book.

7 walk (*verb*)

8 flower

9 serious

10 pretty

11 teacher

12 nice

13 virtue

14 angry

15 crime

Exercise 18.8   *LBCH 18b*
Using prepositions in idioms

In the paragraph below, insert the preposition that correctly completes each idiom. Consult the box in Chapter 18 or a dictionary as needed.

*1 The friend who introduced Nick and Lana was proud _____

his matchmaking. ***2** They had fallen _____ love _____ their first

date. **3** Nick and Lana soon became so dependent _____ each other

that they talked _____ the phone several times every day. **4** Certain

_____ their love, Nick and Lana decided to get married. **5** Now, as

they waited _____ the justice of the peace, they seemed oblivious

_____ the other people in the lobby. **6** But Nick inferred _____

Lana's glance at a handsome man that she was no longer occupied

_____ him alone. **7** Angry _____ Lana, Nick charged her _____ not

loving him enough to get married. **8** Impatient _____ Nick's childish

*Sample answer provided at the back of the book.

behavior, Lana disagreed _____ his interpretation of her glance. **9**

They decided that if they could differ so violently _____ a minor inci-

dent, they should part _____ each other _____ at least a week. **10**

They agreed to think _____ their expectations for marriage.

Exercise 18.9   LBCH 18b
Using prepositions in idioms

Complete the following paragraph by filling in the blanks with the
appropriate prepositions.

*1 The Eighteenth Amendment _____ the US Constitution was

ratified _____ 1919. **2** It prohibited the "manufacture, sale, or trans-

portation _____ intoxicating liquors." **3** Temperance groups _____

the United States wanted to prevent drinking, but the more striking

effect of Prohibition was the boost it gave to organized crime. **4** Ac-

cording _____ legend, the most smuggling and bootlegging oc-

curred _____ Chicago. **5** There, _____ February 14, 1929, Al

Capone gained control _____ the Chicago underworld by ordering

the execution _____ his rival Bugsy Moran and his men _____ a

city parking garage. **6** Though Moran escaped unharmed, Capone

ruled Chicago _____ two bloody years before he was convicted of

tax evasion _____ 1931.

*Sample answer provided at the back of the book.

Exercise 18.10   LBCH 18b
Using figurative language

Invent appropriate similes or metaphors of your own to describe each scene or quality below, and use the figure in a sentence.

Example:
The attraction of a lake on a hot day
The small waves like fingers beckoned us irresistibly.

*1 The sound of a kindergarten classroom

 2 People waiting in line to buy tickets to a rock concert

 3 The politeness of strangers meeting for the first time

 4 A streetlight seen through dense fog

 5 The effect of watching television for ten hours straight

Exercise 18.11   LBCH 18b
Revising: Trite expressions

Revise the following paragraph to eliminate trite expressions.

*Sample answer provided at the back of the book.

*1 The disastrous consequences of the war have shaken the small nation to its roots. 2 Prices for food have shot sky high, and citizens have sneaking suspicions that others are making a killing on the black market. 3 Medical supplies are so few and far between that even civilians who are sick as dogs cannot get treatment. 4 With most men fighting or injured or killed, women have had to bite the bullet and shoulder the burden in farming and manufacturing. 5 Last but not least, the war's heavy drain on the nation's pocketbook has left the economy in shambles.

Exercise 19.1 Revising: Completeness   LBCH 19

Add words to the following paragraph so that the sentences are complete and clear.

*1 The first ice cream, eaten China in about 2000 BC, was lumpier than modern ice cream. 2 The Chinese made their ice cream of milk, spices, and overcooked rice and packed in snow to solidify. 3 Ice milk and fruit ices became popular among wealthy in fourteenth-century

*Sample answer provided at the back of the book.

Italy. 4 At her wedding in 1533 to king of France, Catherine de Médi-

cis offered several flavors of fruit ices. 5 Modern sherbets resemble her

ices; modern ice cream her soft dessert of thick, sweetened cream.

Exercise 20.1 Revising: Writing concisely   LBCH 20

Make the following paragraph more concise. Combine sentences when doing so reduces wordiness.

*If sore muscles after exercising are a problem for you, there are

some measures that can be taken by you to ease the discomfort. *It is

advisable to avoid heat for the first day of soreness. *The application

of heat within the first twenty-four hours can cause an increase in mus-

cle soreness and stiffness. In contrast, the immediate application of

cold will help to reduce inflammation. Blood vessels are constricted by

cold. Blood is kept away from the injured muscles. There are two ways

the application of cold can be made: you can take a cold shower or

use an ice pack. Inflammation of muscles can also be reduced with

aspirin, ibuprofen, or another anti-inflammatory medication. When

*Sample answer provided at the back of the book.

healing is occurring, you need to take it easy. A day or two after over-

doing exercise, it is advisable for you to get some light exercise and

gentle massage.

Exercise 20.2 Revising: Conciseness   **LBCH 20**

Make the following paragraph as concise as possible. Be merciless.

*At the end of a lengthy line of reasoning, he came to the con-

clusion that the situation with carcinogens [cancer-causing sub-

stances] should be regarded as similar to the situation with the

automobile. Instead of giving in to an irrational fear of cancer, we

should consider all aspects of the problem in a balanced and dispas-

sionate frame of mind, making a total of the benefits received from

potential carcinogens (plastics, pesticides, and other similar prod-

ucts) and measuring said total against the damage done by such

products. This is the nature of most discussions about the automo-

bile. Instead of responding irrationally to the visual, aural, and air

*Sample answer provided at the back of the book.

pollution caused by automobiles, we have decided to live with them

(while simultaneously working to improve on them) for the benefits

brought to society as a whole.

PART 4

Sentence Parts and Patterns

Basic Grammar

Exercise 21.1   *LBCH 21a, 21b, 21c*
Identifying nouns, pronouns, and verbs

Identify the words that function as nouns (N), pronouns (P), and verbs (V) in the following paragraph.

Example:

  N   N   V   N

<u>Ancestors</u> of the gingko <u>tree</u> <u>lived</u> 175 to 200 million <u>years</u> ago.

*1 The gingko tree has another name: it is the maidenhair tree. ***2**

Gingko trees sometimes grow to over a hundred feet in height. **3** They

have fan-shaped leaves about three inches wide. **4** A deciduous tree, the

gingko loses its leaves in the fall after they turn bright yellow. **5** Because

the gingko shows tolerance for smoke, low temperatures, and low rain-

fall, it appears in many cities. **6** A shortcoming, however, is the foul odor

*Sample answer provided at the back of the book.

of its fruit. **7** The fruit looks something like a plum. **8** Inside the fruit lies a

large white seed that some Asians value as food. **9** The gingko tree is es-

teemed in the United States and Europe as an ornamental tree. **10** The

male is more common for this purpose because it does not bear fruit.

Exercise 21.2   *LBCH 21d*
Identifying adjectives and adverbs

Identify the adjectives (ADJ) and adverbs (ADV) in the following
paragraph. Mark *a, an,* and *the* as adjectives.

> *Example:*
>
>   ADV
> Stress can hit people when they least expect it.

*1 You can reduce stress by making a few simple changes. ***2** Get

up fifteen minutes earlier than you ordinarily do. **3** Eat a healthy break-

fast, and eat it slowly so that you enjoy it. **4** Do your unpleasant tasks

early in the day. **5** Carry a book or magazine when you know you'll

have to wait in line somewhere. **6** Make promises sparingly and keep

them faithfully. **7** Plan ahead to prevent stressful situations—for exam-

ple, carrying spare keys so you won't be locked out of your car or

*Sample answer provided at the back of the book.

house. **8** See a doctor and dentist regularly. **9** And every day, do at least

one thing you really enjoy.

Exercise 21.3   *LBCH 21e*
Adding connecting words

Fill each blank in the following paragraph with the appropriate connecting word: a preposition, a subordinating conjunction, or a coordinating conjunction. Consult the lists in Chapter 21 if you need help.

> *Example:*
> A Trojan priest warned, "Beware _____ Greeks bearing gifts."
> (*preposition*)
> A Trojan priest warned, "Beware <u>of</u> Greeks bearing gifts."

*1 Just about everyone has heard the story _____ the Trojan

Horse. (*preposition*) ***2** This incident happened at the city of Troy

_____ was planned by the Greeks. (*coordinating conjunction*) **3** The

Greeks built a huge wooden horse; _____ it was a hollow space big

enough to hold many men. (*preposition*) **4** At night, they rolled the

horse to the gate of Troy _____ left it there before sailing their ships

out to sea. (*coordinating conjunction*) **5** _____ the morning, the Tro-

jans were surprised to see the enormous horse. (*preposition*) **6** _____

they were amazed when they saw that the Greeks were gone.

(*coordinating conjunction*) **7** _____ they were curious to examine this

*Sample answer provided at the back of the book.

gift from the Greeks, they dragged the horse into the city and left it outside the temple. (*subordinating conjunction*) **8** In the middle of the night, the hidden Greeks emerged _____ the horse and began setting fires all over town. (*preposition*) **9** _____ the Trojan soldiers awoke and came out of their houses, the Greeks killed them one by one. (*subordinating conjunction*) **10** By the next morning, the Trojan men were dead _____ the women were slaves to the Greeks. (*coordinating conjunction*)

Exercise 22.1   *LBCH 22a*
Identifying subjects and predicates

Identify the subject and the predicate of each sentence below. Then use each sentence as a model to create a sentence of your own.

Example:

subject   predicate
An important scientist | spoke at commencement.
Sample imitation: The hungry family ate at the diner.

*1 The leaves fell.

2 October ends soon.

3 The orchard owners made apple cider.

4 They examined each apple carefully before using it.

5 Over a hundred people will buy cider at the roadside stand.

Exercise 22.2   *LBCH 22a*
Identifying subjects and predicates

In the following sentences, insert a slash between the complete subject and the complete predicate. Underline each simple subject once and each simple predicate twice.

Example:
The <u>pony</u>, the light <u>horse</u>, and the draft <u>horse</u> / <u><u>are</u></u> the three main types of domestic horses.

*1 The horse has a long history of serving humanity but today is mainly a show and sport animal. *2 A member of the genus *Equus,* the domestic horse is related to the wild Przewalski's horse, the ass, and the zebra. 3 The domestic horse and its relatives are all plains-dwelling herd animals. 4 Oddly, the modern horse evolved in North America and then became extinct here after spreading to other parts of the

*Sample answer provided at the back of the book.

world. **5** It was reintroduced here by the Spaniards, profoundly affect-

ing the culture of Native Americans. **6** The North American animals

called wild horses are actually descended from escaped domesticated

horses that reproduced in the wild. **7** According to records, horses

were hunted and domesticated as early as four to five thousand years

ago. **8** The earliest ancestor of the modern horse may have been eo-

hippus, approximately 55 million years ago.

Exercise 22.3   *LBCH 22b*
Identifying sentence parts

In the following sentences identify the subject (S) and verb (V) as
well as any direct object (DO), indirect object (IO), subject complement (SC), or object complement (OC).

Example:

        S   V   V   DO
Crime statistics can cause surprise.

*1 The number of serious crimes in the United States decreased.

*2 A decline in serious crimes occurred each year.

3 The Crime Index measures serious crime.

4 The FBI invented the index.

5 The four serious violent crimes are murder, robbery, forcible rape, and aggravated assault.

6 Auto theft, burglary, arson, and larceny-theft are the four serious crimes against property.

7 The Crime Index gives the FBI a measure of crime.

8 The index shows trends in crimes and the people who commit them.

9 The nation's largest cities showed the largest decline in crime.

10 Smaller cities, where crime did not decrease, proved that the decline in crime is unrepresentative of the nation.

Exercise 22.4   *LBCH 22b*
Identifying sentence patterns

In the following sentences, identify each verb as intransitive, transitive, or linking. Then identify each direct object (DO), indirect object (IO), subject complement (SC), and object complement (OC).

Example:

                transitive
                verb   IO   DO   DO
    Children give their parents both headaches and pleasures.

*1 Many people find New York City exciting.

---

*Sample answer provided at the back of the book.

2 Tourists flock there each year.

3 Often they visit Times Square first.

4 The square's lights are astounding.

5 The flashing signs sell visitors everything from TVs to underwear.

Exercise 23.1   LBCH 23a
Identifying prepositional phrases

Underline the prepositional phrases in the following passage, and name the word that the phrase modifies.

Example:

After an hour I finally arrived at the home of my professor.

*1 On July 3, 1863, at Gettysburg, Pennsylvania, General Robert E.

Lee gambled unsuccessfully for a Confederate victory in the American

Civil War. ***2** Called Pickett's Charge, the battle was one of the most

disastrous conflicts of the war. **3** Confederate and Union forces faced

each other on parallel ridges separated by almost a mile of open fields.

4 After an artillery bombardment of the Union position, about 12,000

*Sample answer provided at the back of the book.

Confederate infantry marched toward the Union ridge. **5** The Union guns had been silent but suddenly roared, mowing the approaching Confederates. **6** Within an hour, perhaps half of the Confederate soldiers lay wounded or dead.

Exercise 23.2 LBCH 23a
Sentence combining: Prepositional phrases

To practice writing sentences with prepositional phrases, combine each group of sentences below into one sentence that includes one or two prepositional phrases. You will have to add, delete, and rearrange words. Some items have more than one possible answer.

> *Example:*
> I will start working. The new job will pay the minimum wage.
> I will start working <u>at a new job</u> <u>for the minimum wage</u>.

*1 The slow loris protects itself well. Its habitat is Southeast Asia. It possesses a poisonous chemical.

2 To frighten predators, the loris exudes the chemical. The chemical comes from a gland. The gland is on the loris's upper arm.

3 The loris's chemical is highly toxic. The chemical is not like a skunk's spray. Even small quantities of the chemical are toxic.

*Sample answer provided at the back of the book.

4 A tiny dose can affect a human. The dose would get in the mouth. The human would be sent into shock.

5 Predators probably can sense the toxin. They detect it at a distance. They use their nasal organs.

Exercise 23.3   LBCH 23a
Identifying verbals and verbal phrases

The following sentences contain participles, gerunds, and infinitives as well as participial, gerund, and infinitive phrases. Identify each verbal or verbal phrase.

Example:
Laughing, the talk-show host prodded her guest to talk.

*1 Written in 1850 by Nathaniel Hawthorne, *The Scarlet Letter* tells

the story of Hester Prynne. 2 Shunned by the community because of

her adultery, Hester endures loneliness. **3** She is humble enough to

withstand her Puritan neighbors' cutting remarks. **4** Despite the cruel

treatment, the determined young woman refuses to leave her home.

5 By living a life of patience and unselfishness, Hester eventually

becomes the community's angel.

*Sample answer provided at the back of the book.

Exercise 23.4   LBCH 23a
Sentence combining: Verbals and verbal phrases

To practice writing sentences with verbals and verbal phrases, combine each of the following pairs of sentences into one sentence. You will have to add, delete, change, and rearrange words. Each item has more than one possible answer.

Example:

My father took pleasure in mean pranks. For instance, he hid the neighbor's cat.

My father took pleasure in mean pranks such as <u>hiding the neighbor's cat</u>.

*1 Air pollution is a health problem. It affects millions of Americans.

2 The air has been polluted mainly by industries and automobiles. It contains toxic chemicals.

3 Environmentalists pressure politicians. They think politicians should pass stricter laws.

4 Many politicians waver. They are not necessarily against environmentalism.

5 The problems are too complex. They cannot be solved easily.

*Sample answer provided at the back of the book.

Exercise 23.5   *LBCH 23a*
Sentence combining: Absolute phrases

To practice writing sentences with absolute phrases, combine each pair of sentences below into one sentence that contains an absolute phrase. You will have to add, delete, change, and rearrange words.

Example:
The flower's petals wilted. It looked pathetic.
Its petals wilted, the flower looked pathetic.

*1 Geraldine Ferraro's face beamed. She enjoyed the crowd's cheers after her nomination for Vice President.

2 A vacancy had occurred. Sandra Day O'Connor was appointed the first female Supreme Court justice.

3 Her appointment was confirmed. Condoleezza Rice became the first female national security adviser.

4 The midterm elections were over. Nancy Pelosi was elected the first female minority leader of the House of Representatives.

5 The election was won. Elizabeth Dole was a US senator from North Carolina.

*Sample answer provided at the back of the book.

Exercise 23.6
Sentence combining: Appositive phrases

LBCH 23a

Combine each pair of sentences into one sentence that contains an appositive phrase. You will have to delete and rearrange words. Some items have more than one possible answer.

Example:

The largest land animal is the elephant. The elephant is also one of the most intelligent animals.

The largest land animal, the elephant, is also one of the most intelligent animals.

*1 Some people perform amazing feats when they are very young. These people are geniuses from birth.

2 John Stuart Mill was a British philosopher. He had written a history of Rome by age seven.

3 Two great artists began their work at age four. They were Paul Klee and Gustav Mahler.

4 Mahler was a Bohemian composer of intensely emotional works. He was also the child of a brutal father.

5 Paul Klee was a Swiss painter. As a child he was frightened by his own drawings of devils.

*Sample answer provided at the back of the book.

Exercise 23.7
Identifying phrases

LBCH 23a

In the paragraphs below, identify every verbal and appositive and every verbal, appositive, prepositional, and absolute phrase. (All but one of the sentences includes two or more such words and phrases.)

*1 Because of its many synonyms, or words with similar meanings, English can make choosing the right word a difficult task. *2 Borrowing words from early Germanic languages and from Latin, English acquired an unusual number of synonyms. 3 With so many choices, how does a writer decide between *motherly* and *maternal* or among *womanly, feminine,* and *female*?

4 Some people prefer longer and more ornate words to avoid the flatness of short words. 5 Indeed, during the Renaissance a heated debate occurred between the Latinists, favoring Latin words, and the Saxonists, preferring Anglo-Saxon words derived from Germanic roots. 6 Today, students in writing classes are often told to choose the shorter word, usually an Anglo-Saxon derivative. 7 Better advice, wrote William Hazlitt, is the principle of choosing "the best word in common use." 8 Keeping

*Sample answer provided at the back of the book.

this principle in mind, a writer would choose either *womanly*, the Anglo-Saxon word, or *feminine*, a French derivative, according to meaning and situation. **9** Of course, synonyms rarely have exactly the same meaning, usage having created subtle but real differences over time. **10** To take another example, the Old English word *handbook* has a slightly different meaning from the French derivative *manual*, a close synonym.

Exercise 23.8 Identifying clauses   LBCH 23b

Underline the subordinate clauses in the following paragraphs and identify each one as adjective (ADJ), adverb (ADV), or noun (N) by determining how it functions in its sentence.

*1 The Prophet Muhammad, who was the founder of Islam, was born about 570 CE in the city of Mecca. ***2** He grew up in the care of his grandfather and an uncle because both of his parents had died when he was very young. **3** His extended family was part of a powerful Arab tribe that lived in western Arabia. **4** When Muhammad was about forty years old, he had a vision while in a cave outside Mecca. **5** He believed that God had selected him to be the prophet of a true religion

*Sample answer provided at the back of the book.

for the Arab people. **6** Viewed as God's messenger, Muhammad attracted many followers before he lost the support of the clans of Mecca. **7** He and his followers moved to Medina, where they established an organized Muslim community that sometimes clashed with the Meccans and with Jewish clans. **8** Throughout his life Muhammad continued as the religious, political, and military leader of Islam as it spread in Asia and Africa. **9** He continued to have revelations, which are recorded in the sacred book of Muslims, the Koran.

Exercise 23.9   *LBCH 23b*
Sentence combining: Subordinate clauses

To practice writing sentences with subordinate clauses, combine each pair of main clauses into one sentence. Use either subordinating conjunctions or relative pronouns as appropriate, referring to the lists in Chapter 21 if necessary. You will have to add, delete, and rearrange words. Each item has more than one possible answer.

Example:
She did not have her tire irons with her. She could not change her bicycle tire.

<u>Because</u> she did not have her tire irons with her, she could not change her bicycle tire.

*1 Moviegoers expect something. Movie sequels should be as exciting as the original films.

---

*Sample answer provided at the back of the book.

2 A few sequels are good films. Most are poor imitations of the originals.

3 A sequel to a blockbuster film arrives in the theater. Crowds quickly line up to see it.

4 Viewers pay to see the same villains and heroes. They remember these characters fondly.

5 Afterward, viewers often grumble about filmmakers. The filmmakers rehash tired plots and characters.

Exercise 24.1   LBCH 24
Identifying sentence structures

Mark the main clauses and subordinate clauses in the following paragraphs. Then identify each sentence as simple, compound, complex, or compound-complex.

Example:

```
            ┌──────────── main clause ─────────────────┐
The human voice is produced in the larynx, a section of the throat
  ┌──────────── subordinate clause ──────────┐
that has two bands called vocal cords. [Complex.]
```

*1 Our world has many sounds, but they all have one thing in

common. ***2** They are all produced by vibrations. **3** Vibrations make

*Sample answer provided at the back of the book.

the air move in waves, and these sound waves travel to the ear.

4 When the waves enter the ear, the brain has to interpret them.

5 Some sounds are pleasant, and others, which we call noise, are not.

6 Pleasant sounds, such as music, are produced by regular vibrations

at regular intervals. 7 Most noises are produced by irregular vibrations

at irregular intervals; an example is the barking of a dog.

8 Sounds, both pleasant and unpleasant, have frequency and

pitch. 9 When an object vibrates rapidly, it produces high-frequency,

high-pitched sounds. 10 People can hear sounds over a wide range of

frequencies; but many other animals, including dogs and cats, can

hear high frequencies that humans can't.

Verbs

Exercise 25.1 Using irregular verbs   *LBCH 25a*

For each irregular verb in brackets, supply either the past tense or
the past participle, as appropriate, and identify the form you used.

*1 The world population had [grow] by two-thirds of a billion peo-

*Sample answer provided at the back of the book.

ple in less than a decade. *2 Recently it [break] the 6 billion mark. 3

Population experts have [draw] pictures of a crowded future, predict-

ing that the world population may have [slide] up to as many 10 bil-

lion by the year 2050. 4 The supply of food, clean water, and land is

of particular concern. 5 Even though the food supply [rise] in the last

decade, the share to each person [fall]. 6 At the same time the water

supply, which had actually [become] healthier in the twentieth centu-

ry, [sink] in size and quality. 6 Changes in land use [run] nomads and

subsistence farmers off their fields, while the overall number of species

on earth [shrink] by 20 percent.

7 Yet not all the news is bad. 8 Recently some countries have

[begin] to heed these and other problems and to explore how technol-

ogy can be [drive] to help the earth and all its populations. 9 Population

control has [find] adherents all over the world. 10 Crop management

has [take] some pressure off lands with poor soil, allowing their owners

to produce food, while genetic engineering promises to replenish food

*Sample answer provided at the back of the book.

supplies that have [shrink]. **11** Some new techniques for waste process-

ing have [prove] effective. **12** Land conservation programs have [give]

endangered species room to reproduce and thrive.

Exercise 25.2   *LBCH 25b*
Distinguishing between sit/set, lie/lay, rise/raise

Choose the correct verb from the pair given in brackets. Then supply the past tense or past participle, as appropriate.

> *Example:*
> After I washed all the windows, I [lie, lay] down the squeegee and
> then I [sit, set] the table.
> After I washed all the windows, I laid down the squeegee and then
> I set the table.

*1 Yesterday afternoon the child [lie, lay] down for a nap.

2 The child has been [rise, raise] by her grandparents.

3 Most days her grandfather has [sit, set] with her, reading her stories.

4 She has [rise, raise] at dawn most mornings.

*Sample answer provided at the back of the book.

5 Her toys were [lie, lay] on the floor.

Exercise 25.3   LBCH 25c
Using -s and -ed verb endings

CULTURE & LANGUAGE Supply the correct form of each verb in brackets. Be careful to include -s and -ed (or -d) endings where they are needed for standard English.

Example:

Unfortunately, the roof on our new house already [leak].
Unfortunately, the roof on our new house already leaks.

*1 A teacher sometimes [ask] too much of a student. ***2** In high school I was once [punish] for being sick. **3** I had [miss] a week of school because of a serious case of the flu. **4** I [realize] that I would fail a test unless I had a chance to make up the class work, so I [discuss] the problem with the teacher. **5** He said I was [suppose] to make up the work while I was sick. **6** At that I [walk] out of the class. **7** I [receive] a failing grade then, but it did not change my attitude. **8** I [work] harder in the courses that have more understanding teachers. **9** Today I still balk when a teacher [make] unreasonable demands or [expect] miracles.

**Sample answer provided at the back of the book.

Exercise 25.4 Using helping verbs   LBCH 25d

CULTURE LANGUAGE Add helping verbs to the following paragraph where they are needed for standard American English. If a sentence is correct as given, mark the number preceding it.

*1 Each year thousands of new readers been discovering Agatha Christie's mysteries. **2** Christie, a well-loved writer who worked as a nurse during World War I, wrote more than sixty-five detective novels. **3** Christie never expected that her mysteries become as popular as they did. **4** Nor did she anticipate that her play, *The Mousetrap*, be performed for decades. **5** At her death in 1976, Christie been the best-selling English novelist for some time. **6** Her books still selling well to readers who like being baffled.

Exercise 25.5   LBCH 25d
Revising: Helping verbs plus main verbs

CULTURE LANGUAGE Revise the following paragraph so that helping verbs and main verbs are used correctly. If a sentence is correct as given, mark the number preceding it.

*1 A report from the Bureau of the Census has confirm a widening gap between rich and poor. **2** As suspected, the percentage

---

*Sample answer provided at the back of the book.

of people below the poverty level did increased over the last decade. **3** More than 17 percent of the population is make 5 percent of all the income. **4** About 1 percent of the population will keeping an average of $500,000 apiece after taxes. **5** The other 99 percent all together will may retain about $300,000.

Exercise 25.6   *LBCH 25e*
Revising: Verbs plus gerunds or infinitives

CULTURE LANGUAGE ➤ Revise the following paragraph so that gerunds or infinitives are used correctly with verbs. Mark the number preceding any sentence that is correct as given.

*1 Without enough highly trained people to draw on, American businesses risk to lose their competitive edge. **2** In recent years, American business leaders have found that their workers need improving their math and science skills. **3** Some colleges have responded by encouraging more students to choose math or engineering as their major. **4** A program called HELP Wanted challenges students take action on behalf of American competitiveness. **5** Officials who work with this

*Sample answer provided at the back of the book.

program hope increasing the number of math, science, and engineer-

ing majors and providing more job training.

Exercise 25.7   *LBCH 25f*
Revising: Verbs plus particles

CULTURE LANGUAGE ▸ The two- and three-word verbs in the paragraph below are underlined. Some are correct as given, and some are not because they should or should not be separated by other words. Revise the verbs and other words that are incorrect. Consult the lists in Chapter 25 or an ESL dictionary if necessary to determine which verbs are separable.

*1 American movies treat everything from <u>going out with</u> some-

one to <u>making up</u> an ethnic identity. **2** Some filmmakers like to ad-

dress current topics, such as <u>getting</u> in today's world <u>along</u>. **3** Others,

however, <u>stay</u> from serious topics <u>away</u> and choose lighter themes. **4**

Whatever the topic, viewers <u>fill</u> theaters <u>up</u> when a movie is controver-

sial. **5** It seems that filmmakers will <u>keep</u> creating controversy <u>on</u>, try-

ing it <u>out</u> whenever they can. **6** They are always eager to make money

and <u>point</u> their influence <u>out</u> to the public.

---

*Sample answer provided at the back of the book.

Exercise 26.1
Revising: Consistent past tense
LBCH 26d

In the paragraph below, change the tenses of the verbs as needed to maintain consistent simple past tense. If a sentence is correct as given, mark the number preceding it.

*1 The 1960 presidential race between Richard Nixon and John F.

Kennedy was the first to feature a televised debate. *2 Despite his

extensive political experience, Nixon perspires heavily and looks hag-

gard and uneasy in front of the camera. 3 By contrast, Kennedy was

projecting cool poise and providing crisp answers that made him seem

fit for the office of President. 4 The public responded positively to

Kennedy's image. 5 His poll ratings shoot up immediately, while

Nixon's take a corresponding drop. 6 Kennedy won the election by a

close 118,564 votes.

Exercise 26.2
Revising: Consistent present tense
LBCH 26d

In the paragraph below, change the tenses of the verbs as needed to maintain consistent simple present tense. If a sentence is correct as given, mark the number preceding it.

*Sample answer provided at the back of the book.

*1 E. B. White's famous children's novel *Charlotte's Web* is a wonderful story of friendship and loyalty. *2 Charlotte, the wise and motherly spider, decided to save her friend Wilbur, the young and childlike pig, from being butchered by his owner. 3 She made a plan to weave words into her web that described Wilbur. 4 She first weaves "Some Pig" and later presented "Terrific," "Radiant," and "Humble." 5 Her plan succeeded beautifully. 6 She fools the humans into believing that Wilbur was a pig unlike any other, and Wilbur lived.

Exercise 26.3   LBCH 26e
Using correct tense sequence

In the following paragraph, change the tense of each bracketed verb so that it is in correct sequence with other verbs.

*1 Diaries that Adolph Hitler [be] supposed to have written surfaced in Germany. 2 Many people believed that the diaries [be] authentic because a well-known historian [have] declared them so. 3 However, the historian's evaluation was questioned by other authorities, who [call] the diaries forgeries. 4 They claimed, among other things, that the

*Sample answer provided at the back of the book.

paper [be] not old enough to have been used by Hitler. 5 Eventually,

the doubters won the debate because they [have] the best evidence.

Exercise 26.4   LBCH 26e
Revising: Tense sequence with conditional sentences

In the following paragraph, use the forms of *be* that create correct tense sequence for all verbs.

*1 If you think you [be] exposed to the flu, you should get a flu shot.

2 You may avoid the illness altogether, and if you contract it your illness

[be] milder. 3 Avoid the vaccine only if you [be] allergic to eggs. 4 If

every person [be] willing and able to get the shot, there [be] very little

serious flu each year. 5 But nearly universal vaccination [be] possible only

if public outreach [be] improved and vaccine supplies [be] adequate.

Exercise 27.1 Revising: Subjunctive mood   LBCH 27

Revise the following paragraph with appropriate subjunctive verb forms. If a sentence is correct as given, mark the number preceding it.

*1 If John Hawkins would have known of all the dangerous side

effects of smoking tobacco, would he have introduced the plant to

*Sample answer provided at the back of the book.

England in 1565? ***2** In promoting tobacco, Hawkins noted that if a Florida Indian man was to travel for several days, he would have smoked tobacco to satisfy his hunger and thirst. **3** Early tobacco growers in the United States feared that their product would not gain acceptance unless it was perceived as healthful, so they spread Hawkins's story. **4** But local governments, more concerned about public safety and morality than health, passed laws requiring that colonists smoked tobacco only if they were five miles from any town. **5** To prevent decadence, in 1647 Connecticut passed a law mandating that one's smoking of tobacco was limited to once a day in one's own home.

Exercise 28.1   *LBCH 28*
Converting between active and passive voices

Convert the verbs in the following sentences from active to passive or from passive to active. (In converting from passive to active, you may need to add a subject.) Which version of the sentence seems more effective and why?

Example:
The aspiring actor was discovered in a nightclub.
A talent <u>scout</u> <u>discovered</u> the actor in a nightclub.

---

*Sample answer provided at the back of the book.

*1 When the Eiffel Tower was built in 1889, it was thought by the French to be ugly.

2 At the time, many people still resisted industrial technology.

3 The tower's naked steel construction typified this technology.

4 Beautiful ornament was expected to grace fine buildings.

5 Further, a structure without solid walls could not even be called a building.

Exercise 28.2   LBCH 28
Revising: Using the active voice

In the following paragraph, rewrite passive sentences into the active voice, adding new sentence subjects as needed.

*1 Water quality is determined by many factors. *2 Suspended and dissolved substances are contained in all natural waters. 3 The amounts of the substances are controlled by the environment. 4 Some

*Sample answer provided at the back of the book.

dissolved substances are produced by pesticides. **5** Other substances,

such as sediment, are deposited in water by fields, livestock feedlots,

and other sources. **6** The bottom life of streams and lakes is affected

by sediment. **7** Light penetration is reduced by sediment, and bottom-

dwelling organisms may be smothered. **8** The quality of water in city

systems is measured frequently. **9** Some contaminants can be removed

by treatment plants. **10** If the legal levels are exceeded by pollutants,

the citizens must be notified by city officials.

Exercise 29.1   **LBCH 29**
Revising: Subject-verb agreement

Revise the verbs in the following paragraphs as needed to make
subjects and verbs agree in number. If a sentence is correct as
given, mark the number preceding it.

*1 Statistics from recent research suggests that humor in the work-

place relieves job-related stress. ***2** Reduced stress in the workplace in

turn reduce illness and absenteeism. ***3** It can also ease friction within

an employee group, which then work together more productively.

*Sample answer provided at the back of the book.

4 Weinstein Associates is a consulting firm that hold workshops designed to make businesspeople laugh. **5** In sessions held by one consultant, each of the participants practice making others laugh. **6** "Isn't there enough laughs within you to spread the wealth?" the consultant asks the students. **7** She quotes Casey Stengel's rule that the best way to keep your management job is to separate the underlings who hate you from the ones who have not decided how they feel. **8** Such self-deprecating comments in public is uncommon among business managers, the consultant says. **9** Each of the managers in a typical firm takes the work much too seriously. **10** The humorous boss often feels like the only one of the managers who have other things in mind besides profits.

11 Another consultant from Weinstein Associates suggest cultivating office humor with practical jokes and cartoons. **12** When a manager or employees drops a rubber fish in the water cooler or posts cartoons on the bulletin board, office spirit usually picks up. **13** If the job of updating the cartoons is entrusted to an employee who has seemed

easily distracted, the employee's concentration often improves. **14**

Even the former sourpuss becomes one of those who hides a bad tem-

per. **15** Every one of the consultants caution, however, that humor has

no place in life-affecting corporate situations such as employee layoffs.

Exercise 29.2   LBCH 29
Adjusting for subject-verb agreement

Rewrite the following paragraphs to change the underlined words
from plural to singular. (You will sometimes need to add *a* or *the*
for the singular, as in the example below.) Then change verbs as
necessary so that they agree with their new subjects.

Example:
Siberian tigers are an endangered subspecies.
The Siberian tiger is an endangered subspecies.

*1 Siberian tigers are the largest living cats in the world, much big-

ger than their relative the Bengal tiger. ***2** They grow to a length of

nine to twelve feet, including their tails, and to a height of about three

and a half feet. ***3** They can weigh over six hundred pounds. **4** These

carnivorous hunters live in northern China and Korea as well as in

**Sample answer provided at the back of the book.

Siberia. **5** During the long winter of this Arctic climate, the yellowish striped <u>coats</u> get a little lighter in order to blend with the snow-covered landscape. **6** The <u>coats</u> also grow quite thick, since the <u>tigers</u> have to withstand temperatures as low as –50°F.

7 <u>Siberian tigers</u> sometimes have to travel great distances to find food. **8** <u>They</u> need about twenty pounds of food a day because of <u>their</u> size and the cold climate, but when <u>they</u> have fresh food <u>they</u> may eat as much as a hundred pounds at one time. **9** <u>They</u> hunt mainly deer, boars, and even bears, plus smaller prey such as fish and rabbits. **10** <u>They</u> pounce on <u>their</u> prey and grab <u>them</u> by the back of the neck. **11** <u>Animals</u> that are not killed immediately are thrown to the ground and suffocated with a bite to the throat. **12** Then the <u>tigers</u> feast.

Pronouns

Exercise 30.1   *LBCH 30a, 30b*
Choosing between subjective and objective pronouns

In the following paragraph, select the appropriate subjective or objective pronoun from the pairs in brackets.

*1 Jody and [I, me] had been hunting for jobs. 2 The best employ-

ees at our old company were [she, her] and [I, me], so [we, us] expect-

ed to find jobs quickly. 3 Between [she, her] and [I, me] the job search

had lasted two months, and still it had barely begun. 4 Slowly, [she,

her] and [I, me] stopped sharing leads. 5 It was obvious that Jody and

[I, me] could not be as friendly as [we, us] had been.

Exercise 30.2   *LBCH 30c*
Choosing between who *and* whom

In the following paragraph, select the appropriate pronoun from
the pairs in brackets.

*1 The school administrators suspended Jurgen, [who, whom]

they suspected of setting the fire. 2 Jurgen had been complaining to

other custodians, [who, whom] reported him. 3 He constantly com-

plained of unfair treatment from [whoever, whomever] happened to

be passing in the halls, including pupils. 4 "[Who, Whom] here has

heard Mr. Jurgen's complaints?" the police asked. 5 "[Who, Whom]

did he complain most about?"

*Sample answer provided at the back of the book.

Exercise 30.3   *LBCH 30c*
Sentence combining: Who *versus* whom

Combine each pair of sentences below into one sentence that contains a clause beginning with *who* or *whom*. Be sure to use the appropriate case form. You will have to add, delete, and rearrange words. Each item may have more than one possible answer.

Example:
David is the candidate. We think David deserves to win.
David is the candidate who we think deserves to win.

*1 Some children have undetected hearing problems. These children may do poorly in school.

2 They may not hear important instructions and information from teachers. Teachers may speak softly.

3 Classmates may not be audible. The teacher calls on those classmates.

4 Some hearing-impaired children may work harder to overcome their disability. These children get a lot of encouragement at home.

5 Some hearing-impaired children may take refuge in fantasy friends. They can rely on these friends not to criticize or laugh.

*Sample answer provided at the back of the book.

Exercise 30.4   LBCH 30d
Choosing between subjective and objective pronouns

In the following paragraph, select the appropriate pronoun from the pairs in brackets.

*1 Obtaining enough protein is important to [we, us] vegetarians.

2 Instead of obtaining protein from meat, [we, us] vegetarians get our protein from other sources such as eggs, cheese, nuts, and beans. 3 Some of [we, us] vegetarians also eat fish, an excellent source of protein, but vegans avoid all animal products, including eggs and cheese. 4 My friend Jeff claims to know only two vegans, Helena and [he, him]. 5 He believes that [we, us] vegetarians who eat fish and dairy products are not as truly vegetarian as [he, him].

Exercise 30.5 Revising: Pronoun case   LBCH 30

Revise all inappropriate case forms in the following paragraph. If a sentence is correct as given, mark the number preceding it.

*1 Written four thousand years ago, *The Epic of Gilgamesh* tells the story of Gilgamesh and his friendship with Enkidu. *2 Gilgamesh was

*Sample answer provided at the back of the book.

a bored king who his people thought was too harsh. *3 Then he met

Enkidu, a wild man whom had lived with the animals in the moun-

tains. 4 Immediately, him and Gilgamesh wrestled to see whom was

more powerful. 5 After hours of struggle, Enkidu admitted that

Gilgamesh was stronger than him. 6 Now the friends needed adven-

tures worthy of them, the two strongest men on earth. 7 Gilgamesh

said, "Between you and I, mighty deeds will be accomplished, and our

fame will be everlasting." 8 Among their acts, Enkidu and him defeat-

ed a giant bull, Humbaba, cut down the bull's cedar forests, and

brought back the logs to Gilgamesh's treeless land. 9 Their heroism

won them great praise from the people. 10 When Enkidu died,

Gilgamesh mourned his death, realizing that no one had been a bet-

ter friend than him. 11 When Gilgamesh himself died many years later,

his people raised a monument praising Enkidu and he for their friend-

ship and their mighty deeds of courage.

*Sample answer provided at the back of the book.

Exercise 31.1   LBCH 31
Revising: Pronoun-antecedent agreement

Revise the following sentences so that pronouns and their antecedents agree in person and number. Try to avoid the generic *he*. If you change the subject of a sentence, be sure to change the verb as necessary for agreement. Mark the number preceding any sentence that is correct as given.

Example:

Each of the Boudreaus' children brought their laundry home at Thanksgiving.

All of the Boudreaus' children brought their laundry home at Thanksgiving. *Or:* Each of the Boudreaus' children brought his or her laundry home at Thanksgiving.

*1 Each girl raised in a Mexican American family in the Rio Grande

Valley of Texas hopes that one day they will be given a *quinceañera*

party for their fifteenth birthday. 2 Such celebrations are very expen-

sive because it entails a religious service followed by a huge party. 3 A

girl's immediate family, unless they are wealthy, cannot afford the

party by themselves. 4 The parents will ask each close friend or relative

if they can help with the preparations. 5 Surrounded by her family and

attended by her friends and their escorts, the *quinceañera* is introduced

as a young woman eligible for Mexican American society.

*Sample answer provided at the back of the book.

Exercise 31.2   LBCH 31
Revising: Pronoun-antecedent agreement

Revise the following sentences so that pronouns and their antecedents agree in person and number. Try to avoid the generic *he*. If you change the subject of a sentence, be sure to change the verb as necessary for agreement. Mark the number preceding any sentence that is correct as given.

*1 Despite their extensive research and experience, neither child psychologists nor parents have yet figured out how children become who they are. *2 Of course, the family has a tremendous influence on the development of a child in their midst. 3 Each member of the immediate family exerts their own unique pull on the child. 4 Other relatives, teachers, and friends can also affect the child's view of the world and of themselves. 5 The workings of genetics also strongly influence the child, but it may never be fully understood. 6 The psychology community cannot agree in its views of whether nurture or nature is more important in a child's development. 7 Another debated issue is whether the child's emotional development or their intellectual development is more central. 8 Just about everyone has their strong

---

opinion on these issues, often backed up by evidence. **9** Neither the

popular press nor scholarly journals devote much of their space to the

wholeness of the child.

Exercise 32.1   LBCH 32a, 32b, 32c, 32d
Revising: Pronoun reference

Rewrite the following paragraph to eliminate unclear pronoun reference. If you use a pronoun in your revision, be sure that it refers to only one antecedent and that it falls close enough to its antecedent to ensure clarity.

*1 There is a difference between the heroes of modern times and

the heroes of earlier times: they have flaws in their characters. **2**

Despite their imperfections, sports fans still admire Pete Rose, Babe

Ruth, and Joe Namath. **3** Fans liked Rose for having his young son

serve as batboy when he was in Cincinnati. **4** The reputation Rose

earned as a gambler and tax evader may overshadow his reputation as

a ballplayer, but it will survive. **5** He amassed an unequaled record as

a hitter, using his bat to do things no one has ever done, and it

remains even though Rose was banned from baseball.

*Sample answer provided at the back of the book.

Exercise 32.2   LBCH 32a, 32b, 32c, 32d
Revising: Pronoun reference

Revise the following paragraph as needed so that pronouns refer to specific, appropriate antecedents. If a sentence is correct as given, mark the number preceding it.

*1 In Charlotte Brontë's *Jane Eyre*, she is a shy young woman who takes a job as a governess. **2** Her employer, a rude, brooding man named Rochester, lives in a mysterious mansion on the English moors, which contributes a strange quality to Jane's experience. **3** Stranger still are the fires, eerie noises, and other unexplained happenings in the house; but Rochester refuses to discuss this. **4** Eventually, they fall in love, but the day they are to marry, she learns that he has a wife hidden in the house. **5** She is hopelessly insane and violent and must be guarded at all times, which explains his strange behavior. **6** Heartbroken, Jane leaves the moors, and many years pass before they are reunited.

Exercise 32.3   LBCH 32f
Revising: Consistency in pronouns

Revise the following paragraph to make pronouns consistent.

*1 When a taxpayer is waiting to receive a tax refund from the Internal Revenue Service, you begin to notice what time the mail carrier arrives. 2 If the taxpayer does not receive a refund check within six weeks of filing a return, they may not have followed the rules of the IRS. 3 For instance, if a taxpayer does not include a Social Security number on a return, you will have to wait for a refund. 4 If one makes errors on the tax form, they will certainly have to wait and they might be audited, delaying a refund for months or longer. 5 A refund may be held up even if you file on time, because returns received close to the April 15 deadline swamp the IRS.

Exercise 32.4 Revising: Pronoun reference   LBCH 32

Revise the following paragraph as needed so that pronouns are consistent and refer to specific, appropriate antecedents.

*1 "Life begins at forty" is a cliché many people live by, and this may or may not be true. *2 Whether one agrees or not with the cliché, you can cite many examples of people whose public lives began at

*Sample answer provided at the back of the book.

forty. **3** For instance, when she was forty, Pearl Buck's novel *The Good Earth* won the Pulitzer Prize. **4** Kenneth Kanuda, past president of Zambia, was elected to it in 1964, when he was forty. **5** Catherine I became Empress of Russia at age forty, more feared than loved by them. **6** Paul Revere at forty made his famous ride to warn American revolutionary leaders that the British were going to arrest them, which gave the colonists time to prepare for battle. **7** Forty-year-old Nancy Astor joined the British House of Commons in 1919 as its first female member, though they did not welcome her. **8** In 610 CE, Muhammad, age forty, began to have visions that became the foundation of the Muslim faith and still inspire millions of people to practice it.

Modifiers

Exercise 33.1   *LBCH 33a, 33b*
Revising: Adjectives and adverbs

Revise the following paragraph to use adjectives and adverbs appropriately. Mark the number preceding any sentence that is correct as given.

*1 The eighteenth-century essayist Samuel Johnson fared bad in his early life. **2** His family was poor, his hearing was weak, and he received little formal education. **3** After failing as a schoolmaster, Johnson moved to London, where he was finally taken serious as a critic and dictionary maker. **4** Johnson was real surprised when he received a pension from King George III. **5** Thinking about his meeting with the king, Johnson felt proudly that he had not behaved badly in the presence of the king. **6** Now, after living cheap for over twenty years, Johnson finally had enough money to eat and dress good. **7** He spent his time writing and living stylish.

Exercise 33.2   *LBCH 33c*
Using comparatives and superlatives

Write the comparative and superlative forms of each adjective or adverb below. Then use all three forms in your own sentences.

Example:
heavy: heavier (comparative), heaviest (superlative)
The barbells were too <u>heavy</u> for me. The trunk was <u>heavier</u> than I expected. Joe Clark was the <u>heaviest</u> person on the team.

*1 badly

2 steady

3 good

4 well

5 understanding

Exercise 33.3
Revising: Comparisons

Revise the following paragraph as needed to correct the forms of adjectives and adverbs and to make comparisons logical. Mark the number preceding any sentence that is correct as given.

*1 The Brontë sisters—Charlotte, Emily, and Anne—are among the more interesting literary families in English history. 2 Of the three novelists, Charlotte was the older. 3 Critics sometimes dispute whether Charlotte or Emily was more talented. 4 For some readers, Emily's *Wuthering Heights* is among the most saddest stories ever written. 5

*Sample answer provided at the back of the book.

For other readers, Charlotte's *Jane Eyre* made more significant contributions to literature than Emily.

Exercise 33.4   LBCH 33d
Revising: Double negatives

Identify and revise the double negatives in the following paragraph. Each error may have more than one correct revision. Mark the number preceding any sentence that is correct as given.

*1 Interest in books about the founding of the United States is not hardly consistent among Americans: it seems to vary with the national mood. **2** Americans show barely any interest in books about the founders when things are going well in the United States. **3** However, when Americans can't hardly agree on major issues, sales of books about the Revolutionary War era increase. **4** During such periods, one cannot go to no bookstore without seeing several new volumes about John Adams, Thomas Jefferson, and other founders. **5** When Americans feel they don't have nothing in common, their increased interest in the early leaders may reflect a desire for unity.

*Sample answer provided at the back of the book.

Exercise 33.5
Revising: Present and past participles

LBCH 33e

CULTURE LANGUAGE Revise the adjectives in the following paragraph as needed to distinguish between present and past participles. Mark the number preceding any sentence that is correct as given.

*1 Many critics found Alice Walker's novel *The Color Purple* to be a fascinated book, though the reviews were mixed. *2 One otherwise excited critic wished that Walker had deleted the scenes set in Africa. 3 Another critic argued that although the book contained many depressed episodes, the overall effect was pleased. 4 Responding to other readers who had found the book annoyed, this critic pointed out its many surprising qualities. 5 In the end most critics agreed that the book was a pleased novel about the struggles of an African American woman. 6 For many, the movie made from the book was less interested. 7 Some viewers found the entire movie irritated, criticizing it for relying on tired feelings. 8 Other viewers thought that Whoopi Goldberg did an amazed job of creating Celie, the central character.

*Sample answer provided at the back of the book.

9 Some critics congratulated Steven Spielberg, the director, for creating a fulfilling movie.

Exercise 33.6 *Revising:* **A, an,** *and* **the**   *LBCH 33f*

⟨ CULTURE LANGUAGE ⟩ In the following paragraph, identify and revise errors in the use of *a, an,* and *the* with count, noncount, and proper nouns. Mark the number preceding any sentence that is correct as given.

*1 A recent court case has moved some Native Americans to observe that a lot of people want to be the Native Americans now that the tribes have something of the value—namely, gambling casinos. ***2** The man named Stephen Jones claimed to be the Native American in order to open casino in the New York's Catskills region. **3** However, the documents Jones provided to support the claim were questioned by a US Bureau of Indian Affairs. **4** On death certificate for Jones's grandfather, the W for *white* had been changed to an I for *Indian* with the ballpoint pen. **5** The ballpoint pens had not been invented until after a grandfather's death. **6** In addition, Jones provided the 1845 census of Indians in New York, and someone had recently added

*Sample answer provided at the back of the book.

Jones's great-grandfather's name to the list of Indian household heads.

7 Jones, who called himself the Chief Golden Eagle, pled guilty to fil-

ing false documents with Bureau of Indian Affairs.

Exercise 33.7 Revising: Determiners   LBCH 33f

CULTURE LANGUAGE In the following paragraph, identify and revise missing or incorrect determiners. Mark the number preceding any sentence that is correct as given.

*1 Much people love to swim for exercise or just plain fun. 2 Few

swimmers, however, are aware of the possible danger of sharing their

swimming spot with others. 3 These danger has increased in recent

years because of dramatic rise in outbreaks of the parasite cryp-

tosporidium. 4 Swallowing even little water containing cryptosporid-

ium can make anyone sick. 5 Chlorine is used in nearly every public

pools to kill parasites, but the chlorine takes six or seven days to kill

cryptosporidium. 6 Most health authorities advise people to limit

their swimming in public pools and to drink as little of the pool water

as possible.

*Sample answer provided at the back of the book.

Exercise 33.8   *LBCH 33*
Revising: Adjectives and adverbs

Revise the paragraph below to correct errors in the use of adjectives and adverbs.

*1 Americans often argue about which professional sport is better: basketball, football, or baseball. ***2** Basketball fans contend that their sport offers more action because the players are constant running and shooting. **3** Because it is played indoors in relative small arenas, basketball allows fans to be more closer to the action than the other sports. **4** Football fanatics say they don't hardly stop yelling once the game begins. **5** They cheer when their team executes a complicated play good. **6** They roar more louder when the defense stops the opponents in a goal-line stand. **7** They yell loudest when a fullback crashes in for a score. **8** In contrast, the supporters of baseball believe that it is the better sport. **9** It combines the one-on-one duel of pitcher and batter struggling valiant with the tight teamwork of double and triple

*Sample answer provided at the back of the book.

plays. **10** Because the game is played slow and careful, fans can analyze and discuss the manager's strategy.

Exercise 34.1   *LBCH 34a*
Revising: Misplaced modifiers

Revise the following paragraph so that modifiers clearly and appropriately describe the intended words.

*1 People dominate in our society who are right-handed. **2** Hand tools, machines, and doors even are designed for right-handed people. **3** However, nearly 15 percent may be left-handed of the population. **4** Children when they enter kindergarten generally prefer one hand or the other. **5** Parents and teachers should not try to deliberately change a child's preference for the left hand.

Exercise 34.2   *LBCH 34a*
Revising: Misplaced modifiers

Revise the following paragraph so that modifiers clearly and appropriately describe the intended words. Mark the number preceding any sentence that is correct as given.

*Sample answer provided at the back of the book.

*1 Women have contributed much to American culture of significance. 2 For example, during the colonial era Elizabeth Pinckney introduced indigo, the source of a valuable blue dye. 3 Later, Emma Willard founded the Troy Female Seminary, the first institution to provide a college-level education for women in 1821. 4 Mary Lyon founded Mount Holyoke Female Seminary as the first true women's college with directors and a campus who would sustain the college even after Lyon's death. 5 Pauline Wright Davis founded in 1853 *Una*, the first US newspaper that was dedicated to gaining women's rights. 6 Maria Mitchell was the first American woman astronomer who lived from 1818 to 1889. 7 Mitchell's Comet was discovered in 1847, which was named for the astronomer.

Exercise 34.3 Arranging adjectives   LBCH 34a

CULTURE LANGUAGE A group of adjectives follows each sentence below. Arrange the adjectives as needed for appropriate order in English, and place them in the sentence.

Example:

Programs for computer graphics perform _____ chores. (*drafting, many, tedious*)

---

*Sample answer provided at the back of the book.

Programs for computer graphics perform <u>many tedious drafting</u> chores.

*1 _____ researchers are studying image controls for computer graphics. (*several, university*)

2 The controls depend on _____ object connected by wires to the computer. (*T-shaped, hand-sized, a*)

3 The image allows a biochemist to walk into _____ display of a molecule. (*three-dimensional, gigantic, a*)

4 Using _____ gestures, the biochemist can rotate and change the entire image. (*simple, hand*)

5 _____ games also depend on computer graphics. (*computer, all, video*)

6 Even _____ games operate this way. (*sophisticated, flight, simulated*)

Exercise 34.4   *LBCH 34b*
Revising: Dangling modifiers

Revise the sentences in the following paragraph to eliminate any
dangling modifiers. Each item has more than one possible answer.
Mark the number preceding any sentence that is correct as given.

*1 Andrew Jackson's career was legendary in his day. ***2** Starting

with the American Revolution, service as a mounted courier was

Jackson's choice. **3** Though not well educated, a successful career as a

lawyer and judge proved Jackson's ability. **4** Earning the nicknames

"Old Hickory" and "Sharp Knife," Jackson established his military

prowess in the War of 1812. **5** Losing only six dead and ten wounded,

the triumph of the Battle of New Orleans burnished Jackson's reputa-

tion. **6** After putting down raiding parties from Florida, Jackson's victo-

ries helped pressure Spain to cede that territory. **7** While Jackson was

briefly governor of Florida, the US presidency became his goal. **8** With

so many skills and deeds of valor, Jackson's fame led to his election to

the presidency in 1828 and 1832.

Exercise 34.5   *LBCH 34*
Revising: Misplaced and dangling modifiers

Revise the following paragraph to eliminate any misplaced or dangling modifiers.

*1 Central American tungara frogs silence several nights a week their mating croaks. 2 When not croaking, the chance that the frogs will be eaten by predators is reduced. 3 The frogs seem to fully believe in "safety in numbers." 4 They more than likely will croak along with a large group rather than by themselves. 5 By forgoing croaking on some nights, the frogs' behavior prevents the species from "croaking."

Sentence Faults

Exercise 35.1   *LBCH 35*
Identifying and revising sentence fragments

Referring as needed to Chapter 35, apply the tests for completeness to each of the word groups in the following paragraph. If a word group is a complete sentence, mark the number preceding it. If it is a sentence fragment, revise it in two ways: by making it a complete sentence, and by combining it with a main clause written from the information given in other items.

*Sample answer provided at the back of the book.

Example:
And could help. [The word group has a verb (*could help*) but no subject.]
Revised into a complete sentence: And <u>he</u> could help.
Combined with a new main clause: <u>He had money</u> and could help.

*1 In an interesting magazine article about vandalism against works of art. **2** The focus was on the vandals themselves. **3** The motives of the vandals varying widely. **4** Those who harm artwork are usually angry. **5** But not necessarily at the artist or the owner. **6** For instance, a man who hammered at Michelangelo's *Pietà*. **7** And knocked off the Virgin Mary's nose. **8** Because he was angry with the Roman Catholic Church. **9** Which knew nothing of his grievance. **10** Although many damaged works can be repaired. **11** Usually even the most skillful repairs are forever visible.

Exercise 35.2
Revising: Sentence fragments

LBCH 35

Correct any sentence fragment below either by combining it with a complete sentence or by making it a complete sentence. If an item contains no sentence fragment, mark the number preceding it.

---

*Sample answer provided at the back of the book.

Example:

Jujitsu is good for self-protection. Because it enables one to over-come an opponent without the use of weapons.

Jujitsu is good for self-protection because it enables one to over-come an opponent without the use of weapons. *Or:* Jujitsu is good for self-protection. It enables one to overcome an opponent without the use of weapons.

*1 Human beings who perfume themselves. They are not much different from other animals.

*2 Animals as varied as insects and dogs release pheromones. Chemicals that signal other animals.

3 Human beings have a diminished sense of smell. And do not consciously detect most of their own species' pheromones.

4 The human substitute for pheromones may be perfumes. Most common in ancient times were musk and other fragrances derived from animal oils.

5 Some sources say that people began using perfume to cover up the smell of burning flesh. During sacrifices to the gods.

*Sample answer provided at the back of the book.

6 Perfumes became religious offerings in their own right. Being expensive to make, they were highly prized.

7 The earliest historical documents from the Middle East record the use of fragrances. Not only in religious ceremonies but on the body.

8 In the nineteenth century, chemists began synthesizing perfume oils. Which previously could be made only from natural sources.

9 The most popular animal oil for perfume today is musk. Although some people dislike its heavy, sweet odor.

10 Synthetic musk oil would help conserve a certain species of deer. Whose gland is the source of musk.

Exercise 35.3   *LBCH 35*
Revising: Sentence fragments

Revise the following paragraph to eliminate sentence fragments by combining them with main clauses or rewriting them as main clauses.

*Baby red-eared slider turtles are brightly colored. *With bold patterns on their yellowish undershells. *Which serve as a warning to

*Sample answer provided at the back of the book.

predators. The bright colors of skunks and other animals. They signal

that the animals will spray nasty chemicals. In contrast, the turtle's col-

ors warn largemouth bass. That the baby turtle will actively defend it-

self. When a bass gulps down a turtle. The feisty baby claws and bites.

Forcing the bass to spit it out. To avoid a similar painful experience.

The bass will avoid other baby red-eared slider turtles. The turtle loses

its bright colors as it grows too big. For a bass's afternoon snack.

Exercise 36.1   LBCH 36
Identifying and revising comma splices

Correct each comma splice below in *two* of the ways described in
Chapter 36. If a sentence contains no comma splice, mark the
number preceding it.

*1 Money has a long history, it goes back at least as far as the ear-

liest records. 2 Many of the earliest records concern financial transac-

tions, indeed, early history must often be inferred from commercial

activity. 3 Every known society has had a system of money, though the

objects serving as money have varied widely. 4 Sometimes the objects

*Sample answer provided at the back of the book.

had actual value for the society, examples include cattle and ferment-

ed beverages. **5** Today, in contrast, money may be made of worthless

paper, or it may even consist of a bit of data in a computer's memory.

6 We think of money as valuable, only our common faith in it makes it

valuable. **7** That faith is sometimes fragile, consequently, currencies

themselves are fragile. **8** Economic crises often shake the belief in

money, indeed, such weakened faith helped cause the Great

Depression of the 1930s.

Exercise 36.2   *LBCH 36*
Identifying and revising fused sentences

Revise each of the fused sentences in the paragraph below in *two* of
the four ways shown in Chapter 36. If a sentence is correct as
given, mark the number preceding it.

*1 Throughout history money and religion were closely linked

there was little distinction between government and religion. **2** The

head of state and the religious leader were often the same person so

that all power rested in one ruler. **3** These powerful leaders decided

*Sample answer provided at the back of the book.

what objects would serve as money their backing encouraged public faith in the money. **4** Coins were minted of precious metals the religious overtones of money were then strengthened. **5** People already believed the precious metals to be divine their use in money intensified its allure.

Exercise 36.3   *LBCH 36*
Sentence combining: Comma splices and fused sentences

Using the method suggested in parentheses, combine each pair of sentences below into one sentence without creating a comma splice or fused sentence.

Example:
The sun sank lower in the sky. The colors gradually faded. (*Subordinate one clause to the other.*)
As the sun sank lower in the sky, the colors gradually faded.

*1 The exact origin of paper money is unknown. It has not survived as coins, shells, and other durable objects have. (*Subordinate one clause to the other.*)

2 Scholars disagree over where paper money originated. Many believe it was first used in Europe. (*Subordinate one clause to the other.*)

*Sample answer provided at the back of the book.

3 Perhaps goldsmiths were also gold bankers. They held the gold of their wealthy customers. (*Supply a semicolon and a conjunctive adverb or transitional expression.*)

4 The goldsmiths probably gave customers receipts for their gold. These receipts were then used in trade. (*Supply a comma and coordinating conjunction.*)

5 The goldsmiths were something like modern-day bankers. Their receipts were something like modern-day money. (*Supply a semicolon.*)

Exercise 36.4   *LBCH 36*
Revising: Comma splices and fused sentences

Revise each comma splice and fused sentence in the following paragraphs using the technique that seems most appropriate for the meaning.

*What many call the first genocide of modern times occurred

during World War I, the Armenians were deported from their homes

in Anatolia, Turkey. The Turkish government assumed that the Ar-

menians were sympathetic to Russia, with whom the Turks were at

*Sample answer provided at the back of the book.

war. Many Armenians died because of the hardships of the journey,

many were massacred. The death toll was estimated at between

600,000 and 1 million.

Many of the deported Armenians migrated to Russia, in 1918

they established the Republic of Armenia, they continued to be

attacked by Turkey, in 1920 they became the Soviet Republic of

Armenia rather than surrender to the Turks. Like other Soviet

republics, Armenia became independent in 1991, about 3.4 million

Armenians live there now.

Exercise 37.1   *LBCH 37a, 37b*
Revising: Mixed sentences

Revise the following paragraph so that sentence parts fit together
both in grammar and in meaning. Each item has more than one
possible answer. If a sentence is correct as given, mark the number
preceding it.

*1 A hurricane is when the winds in a tropical depression rotate

counterclockwise at more than seventy-four miles per hour. *2 People

fear hurricanes because they can destroy lives and property. 3 Through

*Sample answer provided at the back of the book.

storm surge, high winds, floods, and tornadoes is how hurricanes have killed thousands of people. **4** Storm surge is where the hurricane's winds whip up a tide that spills over seawalls and deluges coastal islands. **5** The winds themselves are also destructive, uprooting trees and smashing buildings. **6** By packing winds of 150 to 200 miles per hour is how a hurricane inflicts terrible damage even on inland towns. **7** However, the worst damage to inland areas occurs when tornadoes and floods strike. **8** Many scientists observe that hurricanes in recent years they have become more ferocious and destructive. **9** However, in the last half-century, with improved communication systems and weather satellites have made hurricanes less deadly. **10** The reason is because people have more time to escape. **11** The emphasis on evac-uation is in fact the best way for people to avoid a hurricane's force. **12** Simply boarding up a house's windows will not protect a family from wind, water surges, and flying debris.

Exercise 37.2
Revising: Repeated subjects and other parts

LBCH 37c

＊ CULTURE LANGUAGE ＞ Revise the sentences in the following paragraph to eliminate any unneeded words. If a sentence is correct as given, mark the number preceding it.

*1 Archaeologists and other scientists they can often determine the age of their discoveries by means of radiocarbon dating. 2 This technique is based on the fact that all living organisms contain carbon. 3 The most common isotope is carbon 12, which it contains six protons and six neutrons. 4 A few carbon atoms are classified as the isotope carbon 14, where the nucleus consists of six protons and eight neutrons there. 5 Because of the extra neutrons, the carbon 14 atom it is unstable. 6 What is significant about the carbon 14 atom is its half-life of 5700 years. 7 Scientists they measure the proportion of carbon 14 to carbon 12 and estimate the age of the specimen. 8 Radiocarbon dating it can be used on any material that was once living, but it is most accurate with specimens between 500 and 50,000 years old.

PART 5

Punctuation

Exercise 38.1 Revising: Periods   **LBCH 38a**

Revise the following sentences so that periods are used correctly.

*1 The instructor asked when Plato wrote *The Republic*?

2 Give the date within one century

3 The exact date is not known, but it is estimated at 370 BCE

4 Dr Arn will lecture on Plato at 7:30 p.m..

5 The area of the lecture hall is only 1600 sq ft

Exercise 38.2   **LBCH 38b**
Revising: Question marks

Add, delete, or replace question marks as needed in the following sentences.

*1 In Homer's *Odyssey*, Odysseus took several years to travel from Troy to Ithaca. Or was it eight years. Or more?

*Sample answer provided at the back of the book.

2 Odysseus must have wondered whether he would ever make it home?

3 "What man are you and whence?," asks Odysseus's wife Penelope.

4 Why does Penelope ask, "Where is your city? Your family?"?

5 Penelope does not recognize Odysseus and asks who this stranger is?

Exercise 38.3   LBCH 38c
Revising: Exclamation points

Add or replace exclamation points as needed in the following sentences.

*1 As the firefighters moved their equipment into place, the police shouted, "Move back!".

2 A child's cries could be heard from above: "Help me. Help."

3 When the child was rescued, the crowd called "Hooray."

4 The rescue was the most exciting event of the day!

5 The neighbors talked about it for days!

*Sample answer provided at the back of the book.

Exercise 38.4 Revising: End punctuation   LBCH 38

Insert appropriate end punctuation (periods, question marks, or exclamation points) where needed in the following paragraph.

*When visitors first arrive in Hawaii, they often encounter an unexpected language barrier *Standard English is the language of business and government, but many of the people speak Pidgin English Instead of an excited "Aloha" the visitors may be greeted with an excited Pidgin "Howzit" or asked if they know "how fo' find one good hotel" Many Hawaiians question whether Pidgin will hold children back because it prevents communication with *haoles,* or Caucasians, who run businesses Yet many others feel that Pidgin is a last defense of ethnic diversity on the islands To those who want to make standard English the official language of the state, these Hawaiians may respond, "Just 'cause I speak Pidgin no mean I dumb" They may ask, "Why you no listen" or, in standard English, "Why don't you listen"

*Sample answer provided at the back of the book.

Exercise 39.1   *LBCH 39a*
Revising: Comma with linked main clauses

In the following paragraph, insert a comma before each coordinating conjunction that links main clauses. Do not insert commas between words, phrases, or subordinate clauses. If a sentence is correct as given, mark the number preceding it.

*1 Parents once automatically gave their children the father's last name but some no longer do. **2** In fact, parents were once legally required to give their children the father's last name but these laws have been contested in court. **3** Parents may now give their children any last name they choose and some parents opt for the mother's last name. **4** Those parents who choose the mother's last name may do so because they believe the mother's importance should be recognized or because the mother's name is easier to pronounce.

Exercise 39.2   *LBCH 39a*
Sentence combining: Linked main clauses

Combine each group of sentences below into one sentence that contains only two main clauses connected by the coordinating conjunction in parentheses. Use commas only to separate the main clauses. You will have to add, delete, and rearrange words.

*Sample answer provided at the back of the book.

Example:
The circus had come to town. The children wanted to see it. Their parents wanted to see it. (*and*)
The circus had come to town, <u>and</u> the children and their parents wanted to see it.

*1 The arguments for bestowing the mother's surname on children are often strong. They are often convincing. They are not universally accepted. (*but*)

2 Some parents have combined their last names. They have created a new surname. They have given that name to their children. (*and*)

3 Critics sometimes question the effects of unusual surnames on children. They wonder how confusing the new surnames will be. They wonder how fleeting the surnames will be. (*or*)

4 Children with surnames different from their parents' may suffer embarrassment. They may suffer identity problems. Giving children their father's surname is still very much the norm. (*for*)

5 Hyphenated names are awkward. They are also difficult to pass on. Some observers think they will die out in the next generation. Or they may die out before. (*so*)

*Sample answer provided at the back of the book.

Exercise 39.3   LBCH 39b
Revising: Comma with introductory elements

In the following paragraph, insert commas wherever they are needed after introductory elements. If a sentence is correct as given, mark the number preceding it.

*1 Veering sharply to the right a large flock of birds neatly avoids

a high wall. ***2** Moving in a fluid mass is typical of flocks of birds and

schools of fish. **3** With the help of complex computer simulations zo-

ologists are learning more about this movement. **4** Because it is sud-

den and apparently well coordinated the movement of flocks and

schools has seemed to be directed by a leader. **5** Almost incredibly

the group could behave with more intelligence than any individual

seemed to possess. **6** However new studies have discovered that

flocks and schools are leaderless. **7** As it turns out evading danger is

really an individual response. **8** When each bird or fish senses a pred-

ator it follows individual rules for fleeing. **9** To keep from colliding

with its neighbors each bird or fish uses other rules for dodging. **10**

*Sample answer provided at the back of the book.

Multiplied over hundreds of individuals these responses look as if they

have been choreographed.

Exercise 39.4   *LBCH 39b*
Sentence combining: Introductory elements

Combine each pair of sentences below into one sentence that begins with an introductory modifier as specified in parentheses. Follow the introductory element with a comma. You will have to add, delete, change, and rearrange words.

Example:

The girl was humming to herself. She walked upstairs. (*Modifier beginning Humming.*)

Humming to herself, the girl walked upstairs.

*1 Scientists have made an effort to explain the mysteries of flocks and schools. They have proposed bizarre magnetic fields and telepathy. (*Modifier beginning In.*)

2 Scientists developed computer models. They have abandoned earlier explanations. (*Modifier beginning Since.*)

3 The movement of a flock or school starts with each individual. It is rapidly and perhaps automatically coordinated among individuals. (*Modifier beginning Starting.*)

*Sample answer provided at the back of the book.

4 One zoologist observes that human beings seek coherent patterns. He suggests that investigators saw purpose in the movement of flocks and schools where none existed. (*Modifier beginning* <u>*Observing.*</u>)

5 One may want to study the movement of flocks or schools. Then one must abandon a search for purpose or design. (*Modifier beginning* <u>To</u>.)

Exercise 39.5   LBCH 39c
Revising: Punctuation of nonessential and essential elements

Insert commas as needed in the following paragraph to set off nonessential elements, and delete any commas that incorrectly set off essential elements. If a sentence is correct as given, mark the number preceding it.

*1 Anesthesia which is commonly used during medical operations once made patients uncomfortable and had serious risks. ***2** But new drugs and procedures, that have been developed in recent years, allow patients under anesthesia to be comfortable and much safer. **3** Twenty years ago, any patient, undergoing anesthesia, would have had to stay overnight in a hospital, probably feeling sick and very con-

---

*Sample answer provided at the back of the book.

fused. **4** Many patients can have general anesthesia, which renders them completely unconscious, and still go home the same day. **5** Another form of anesthesia, monitored anesthesia or conscious sedation, allows the patient to be awake while feeling sleepy with no pain. **6** A surgeon may also suggest regional or local anesthesia which numbs only a specific part of the body and leaves the patient completely awake. **7** Sometimes, patients must choose among local, regional, and general anesthesia whether or not they want to make the choice. **8** In that case, patients should ask which type the anesthesiologist would choose if his or her child or spouse were having the surgery.

Exercise 39.6   *LBCH 39c*
Revising: Punctuation of nonessential
and essential elements

Insert commas as needed in the following paragraphs to set off nonessential elements, and delete any commas that incorrectly set off essential elements. If a sentence is correct as given, mark the number preceding it.

*1 Italians insist that Marco Polo the thirteenth-century explorer did not import pasta from China. ***2** Pasta which consists of flour and

*Sample answer provided at the back of the book.

water and often egg existed in Italy long before Marco Polo left for his

travels. **3** A historian who studied pasta says that it originated in the

Middle East in the fifth century. **4** Most Italians dispute this account al-

though their evidence is shaky. **5** Wherever it originated, the Italians

are now the undisputed masters, in making and cooking pasta.

6 Marcella Hazan, who has written several books on Italian cooking,

insists that homemade and hand-rolled pasta is the best. **7** However,

most cooks buy dried pasta lacking the time to make their own. **8**

Homemade or dried, the finest pasta is made from semolina, a flour

from hard durum wheat. **9** Pasta manufacturers choose hard durum

wheat, because it makes firmer cooked pasta than common wheat does.

10 Pasta, made from common wheat, gets soggy in boiling water.

Exercise 39.7   *LBCH 39c*
Sentence combining: Essential and nonessential elements

Combine each pair of sentences below into one sentence that uses
the element described in parentheses. Insert commas as appropriate. You will have to add, delete, change, and rearrange words.
Some items have more than one possible answer.

Example:

Mr. Ward's oldest sister helped keep him alive. She was a nurse in the hospital. (*Nonessential clause beginning who*.)

Mr. Ward's oldest sister, <u>who was a nurse in the hospital</u>, helped keep him alive.

*1 American colonists first imported pasta from the English. The English had discovered it as tourists in Italy. (*Nonessential clause beginning <u>who</u>.*)

2 The English returned from their grand tours of Italy. They were called *macaronis* because of their fancy airs. (*Essential phrase beginning <u>returning</u>.*)

3 A hair style was also called *macaroni*. It had elaborate curls. (*Essential phrase beginning <u>with</u>.*)

4 The song "Yankee Doodle" refers to this hairdo. It reports that Yankee Doodle "stuck a feather in his cap and called it macaroni." (*Essential clause beginning <u>when</u>.*)

5 The song was actually intended to poke fun at unrefined American colonists. It was a creation of the English. (*Nonessential appositive beginning <u>a creation</u>.*)

Exercise 39.8
Revising: Commas with series items

LBCH 39d

In the following paragraph, insert commas as needed to punctuate items in a series. If a sentence is correct as given, mark the number preceding it.

*1 Photographers who take pictures of flowers need to pay special attention to lighting composition and focal point. **2** Many photographers prefer to shoot in the early morning, when the air is calm, the dew is still on the flowers, and the light is soft. **3** Some even like to photograph in light rain because water helps flowers to look fresh colorful and especially lively. **4** In composing a picture, the photographer can choose to show several flowers, just one flower or even a small part of a flower. **5** One effective composition leads the viewer's eye in from an edge of the photo devotes a large amount of the photo to the primary subject and then leads the eye out of the photo. **6** The focus changes as the eye moves away from the subject: the primary subject is in sharp focus, elements near the primary subject are in sharp focus and elements in the background are deliberately out of focus.

*Sample answer provided at the back of the book.

Exercise 39.9   LBCH 39e
Revising: Commas with adjectives

In the following paragraph, insert commas as needed between adjectives, and delete any unneeded commas. If a sentence is correct as given, mark the number preceding it.

*1 Most people have seen a blind person being aided by a patient

observant guide dog. 2 What is not commonly known is how normal

untrained dogs become these special, highly skilled dogs. 3 An organ-

ization called the Seeing Eye breeds dogs to perform this specific,

guide job. 4 Enthusiastic affectionate volunteers raise the dogs until

they are about seventeen months old. 5 Each dog then undergoes a

thorough health examination. 6 Dogs who pass the health exam go

through a rigorous, four-month, training program. 7 The trained dog

is then matched with a blind person, and the two of them undergo

their own intensive communication training before graduating to their

life together.

Exercise 39.10   LBCH 39d, 39e
Revising: Punctuation of series and adjectives

Insert commas as needed in the following paragraph to separate series items or adjectives. If a sentence is correct as given, mark the number preceding it.

*1 Shoes with high heels were originally designed to protect the wearer's feet from mud garbage and animal waste in the streets. *2 The first high heels worn strictly for fashion, however, appeared in the sixteenth century. 3 They were made popular when the short powerful King Louis XIV of France began wearing them. 4 At first, high heels were worn by men and were made of colorful silk fabrics soft suedes or smooth leathers. 5 But Louis's influence was so strong that men and women of the court priests and cardinals and even household servants wore high heels. 6 By the seventeenth and eighteenth centuries, only wealthy fashionable French women wore high heels. 7 At that time, French culture represented the one true standard of elegance and re-finement. 8 High-heeled shoes for women spread to other courts of

*Sample answer provided at the back of the book.

Europe among the Europeans of North America and to all social

classes. **9** Now high heels are common, though depending on the

fashion they range from short squat thick heels to tall skinny spikes. **10**

A New York boutique recently showed a pair of purple satin pumps

with tiny jeweled bows and four-inch stiletto heels.

Exercise 39.11   LBCH 39f
Revising: Punctuation of dates, addresses,
place names, numbers

Insert commas as needed in the following paragraph.

*1 The festival will hold a benefit dinner and performance on

March 10 2007 in Asheville. **2** The organizers hope to raise more than

$100000 from donations and ticket sales. **3** Performers are expected

from as far away as Milan Italy and Kyoto Japan. **4** All inquiries sent to

Mozart Festival PO Box 725 Asheville North Carolina 28803 will re-

ceive a quick response. **5** The deadline for ordering tickets by mail is

Monday December 3 2006.

*Sample answer provided at the back of the book.

Exercise 39.12
Revising: Punctuation of quotations

LBCH 39g

In the following sentences, insert commas or semicolons as needed to correct punctuation with quotations. If a sentence is correct as given, mark the number preceding it.

*1 The writer and writing teacher Peter Elbow proposes an "open-ended writing process" that "can change you, not just your words."

2 "I think of the open-ended writing process as a voyage in two stages" Elbow says.

3 "The sea voyage is a process of divergence, branching, proliferation, and confusion" Elbow continues "the coming to land is a process of convergence, pruning, centralizing, and clarifying."

4 "Keep up one session of writing long enough to get loosened up and tired" advises Elbow "long enough in fact to make a bit of a voyage."

5 "In coming to new land" Elbow says "you develop a new conception of what you are writing about."

Exercise 39.13
Revising: Needless and misused commas

LBCH 39h

Revise the following paragraph to eliminate needless or misused commas. If a sentence is correct as given, mark the number preceding it.

*1 One of the largest aquifers in North America, the Ogallala aquifer, is named after the Ogallala Indian tribe, which once lived in the region and hunted buffalo there. ***2** The Ogallala aquifer underlies a region from western Texas through northern Nebraska, and has a huge capacity of fresh water, that is contained in a layer of sand and gravel. **3** But, the water in the Ogallala is being removed faster than it is being replaced. **4** Water is pumped from the aquifer for many purposes, such as, drinking and other household use, industrial use, and, agricultural use. **5** The Great Plains area above the Ogallala, often lacks enough rainfall for the crops, that are grown there. **6** As a consequence, the crops in the Great Plains are watered by irrigation systems, that pump water from the Ogallala, and distribute it from half-mile-long sprinkler arms. **7** Ogallala water is receding between six inches and three feet a year, the amount depending on location. **8** Some areas are experiencing water shortages already, and the pumping continues. **9** A scientific

*Sample answer provided at the back of the book.

commission recently estimated that, "at the present consumption rate,

the Ogallala will be depleted in forty years."

Exercise 39.14 Revising: Commas   **LBCH 39**

Insert commas as needed in the following paragraphs, and delete
any misused commas. If a sentence is correct as given, mark the
number preceding it.

*1 Ellis Island New York reopened for business in 1990 but now the

customers are tourists not immigrants. ***2** This spot which lies in New

York Harbor was the first American soil seen, or touched by many of

the nation's immigrants. ***3** Though other places also served as ports

of entry for foreigners none has the symbolic power of, Ellis Island.

4 Between its opening in 1892 and its closing in 1954, over 20 million

people about two-thirds of all immigrants were detained there before

taking up their new lives in the United States. **5** Ellis Island processed

over 2000 newcomers a day when immigration was at its peak

between 1900 and 1920.

6 As the end of a long voyage and the introduction to the New World Ellis Island must have left something to be desired. **7** The "huddled masses" as the Statue of Liberty calls them indeed were huddled. **8** New arrivals were herded about kept standing in lines for hours or days yelled at and abused. **9** Assigned numbers they submitted their bodies to the pokings and proddings of the silent nurses and doctors, who were charged with ferreting out the slightest sign, of sickness disability or insanity. **10** That test having been passed, the immigrants faced interrogation by an official through an interpreter. **11** Those, with names deemed inconveniently long or difficult to pronounce, often found themselves permanently labeled with abbreviations, of their names, or with the names, of their hometowns. **12** But, millions survived the examination humiliation and confusion, to take the last short boat ride to New York City. **13** For many of them and especially for their descendants Ellis Island eventually became not a nightmare but the place where a new life began.

Exercise 40.1   *LBCH 40a*
Revising: Punctuation between main clauses

In the following paragraph, insert semicolons as needed to separate main clauses. If a sentence is correct as given, mark the number preceding it.

*1 More and more musicians are playing computerized instruments more and more listeners are worrying about the future of acoustic instruments. 2 The computer is not the first technology in music the pipe organ and saxophone were also technological breakthroughs in their day. 3 Musicians have always experimented with new technology while audiences have always resisted the experiments. 4 Most computer musicians are not merely following the latest fad they are discovering new sounds and new ways to manipulate sound. 5 Few musicians have abandoned acoustic instruments most value acoustic sounds as much as electronic sounds.

Exercise 40.2   *LBCH 40b*
Revising: Punctuation between main clauses with conjunctive adverbs or transitional expressions

In the following paragraph, insert semicolons as needed to separate main clauses related by a conjunctive adverb or transitional

*Sample answer provided at the back of the book.

expression. Also insert a comma or commas as needed to set off the adverb or expression.

*1 Music is a form of communication like language the basic elements however are not letters but notes. **2** Computers can process any information that can be represented numerically as a result they can process musical information. **3** A computer's ability to process music depends on what software it can run it must moreover be connected to a system that converts electrical vibration into sound. **4** Computers and their sound systems can produce many different sounds indeed the number of possible sounds is infinite. **5** The powerful music computers are very expensive therefore they are used only by professional musicians.

Exercise 40.3   LBCH 40a, 40b
Sentence combining: Related main clauses

Combine each set of three sentences below into one sentence containing only two main clauses. As indicated in parentheses, connect the clauses with a semicolon alone or with a semicolon plus a conjunctive adverb or transitional expression followed by a comma. You will have to add, delete, change, and rearrange words. Each item has more than one possible answer.

*Sample answer provided at the back of the book.

Example:

The Albanians censored their news. We got little news from them. And what we got was unreliable. (*Therefore and semicolon.*)

The Albanians censored their news; therefore, the little news we got from them was unreliable.

*1 Electronic instruments are prevalent in jazz. They are also prevalent in rock music. They are less common in classical music. (*However and semicolon.*)

2 Jazz and rock change rapidly. They nourish experimentation. They nourish improvisation. (*Semicolon alone.*)

3 The notes and instrumentation of traditional classical music were established by a composer. The composer was writing decades or centuries ago. Such music does not change. (*Therefore and semicolon.*)

4 Contemporary classical music not only can draw on tradition. It can also respond to innovations. These are innovations such as jazz rhythms and electronic sounds. (*Semicolon alone.*)

5 Much contemporary electronic music is more than just one type of music. It is more than just jazz, rock, or classical. It is a fusion of all three. (*Semicolon alone.*)

*Sample answer provided at the back of the book.

Exercise 40.4   *LBCH 40c*
Revising: Punctuation of main clauses
and series items containing commas

Substitute semicolons for commas in the following paragraph to separate main clauses or series items that contain commas.

*1 The Indian subcontinent is separated from the rest of the world by clear barriers: the Bay of Bengal and the Arabian Sea to the east and west, respectively, the Indian Ocean to the south, and 1600 miles of mountain ranges to the north. 2 In the north of India are the world's highest mountains, the Himalayas, and farther south are fertile farmlands, unpopulated deserts, and rain forests. 3 India is a nation of ethnic and linguistic diversity, with numerous religions, including Hinduism, Islam, and Christianity, with distinct castes and ethnic groups, and with sixteen languages, including the official Hindi and the "associate official" English.

Exercise 40.5 Revising: Semicolons   *LBCH 40*

In the following paragraph, insert semicolons as needed and eliminate any misused semicolons, substituting other punctuation as appropriate. If a sentence is correct as given, mark the number preceding it.

*Sample answer provided at the back of the book.

*1 The set, sounds, and actors in the movie captured the essence

of horror films. *2 The set was ideal; dark, deserted streets, trees dip-

ping their branches over the sidewalks, mist hugging the ground and

creeping up to meet the trees, looming shadows of unlighted, turret-

ed houses. 3 The sounds, too, were appropriate, especially terrifying

was the hard, hollow sound of footsteps echoing throughout the film.

4 But the best feature of the movie was its actors; all of them tall, pale,

and thin to the point of emaciation. 5 With one exception, they were

dressed uniformly in gray and had gray hair. 6 The exception was an

actress who dressed only in black as if to set off her pale yellow, near-

ly white, long hair; the only color in the film. 7 The glinting black eyes

of another actor stole almost every scene, indeed, they were the

source of the film's mischief.

Exercise 41.1 Revising: Colons   *LBCH 41*

In the following paragraph, insert colons as needed and delete misused colons. If a sentence is correct as given, mark the number preceding it.

*Sample answer provided at the back of the book.

*1 In remote areas of many developing countries, simple signs mark

human habitation a dirt path, a few huts, smoke from a campfire. **2**

However, in the built-up sections of industrialized countries, nature is all

but obliterated by signs of human life, such as: houses, factories, sky-

scrapers, and highways. **3** The spectacle makes many question the

words of Ecclesiastes 1.4 "One generation passeth away, and another

cometh; but the earth abideth forever." **4** Yet many scientists see the

future differently: they hold that human beings have all the technology

necessary to clean up the earth and restore the cycles of nature. **5** All

that is needed is: a change in the attitudes of those who use technology.

Exercise 41.2   **LBCH 41**
Revising: Colons and semicolons

In the following paragraphs, insert colons and semicolons as
needed and delete or replace them where they are misused. If a
sentence is correct as given, mark the number preceding it.

*1 Sunlight is made up of three kinds of radiation: visible rays;

infrared rays, which we cannot see; and ultraviolet rays, which are also

---

*Sample answer provided at the back of the book.

invisible. *2 Infrared rays are the longest; measuring 700 nanometers

and longer; while ultraviolet rays are the shortest; measuring 400

nanometers and shorter. 3 Especially in the ultraviolet range; sunlight

is harmful to the eyes. 4 Ultraviolet rays can damage the retina: fur-

thermore, they can cause cataracts on the lens.

5 The lens protects the eye by: absorbing much of the ultraviolet

radiation and thus protecting the retina. 6 Protecting the retina, how-

ever, the lens becomes a victim; growing cloudy and blocking vision.

7 The best way to protect your eyes is: to wear hats that shade the face

and sunglasses that screen out ultraviolet rays. 8 Many sunglass lenses

have been designed as ultraviolet screens; many others are extremely

ineffective. 9 If sunglass lenses do not screen out ultraviolet rays and if

people can see your eyes through them, they will not protect your

eyes, and you will be at risk for cataracts later in life. 10 People who

spend much time outside in the sun; owe it to themselves to buy and

wear sunglasses that shield their eyes.

*Sample answer provided at the back of the book.

Exercise 42.1 Forming possessives   *LBCH 42a*

Form the possessive of each word or word group in brackets.

Example:
The [men] blood pressures were higher than the [women].
The men's blood pressures were higher than the women's.

*1 In the myths of ancient Greeks, the [goddesses] roles vary wide-

ly. *2 [Demeter] responsibility is the fruitfulness of the earth. 3 [Athena]

role is to guard the city of Athens. 4 [Artemis] function is to care for

wild animals and small children. 5 [Athena and Artemis] father, Zeus,

is the king of the gods.

6 Even a single [goddess] responsibilities are often varied. 7 For

instance, over several [centuries] time Athena changes from a [mariner]

goddess to the patron of crafts. 8 She is also concerned with fertility

and with [children] well-being, since the strength of Athens depended

on a large and healthy population. 9 Athena often changes into [birds]

forms, and in [Homer] *Odyssey,* she assumes a [sea eagle] form.

10 In ancient Athens the myths of Athena were part of [everyone]

knowledge and life. 11 A cherished myth tells how she fights to retain

*Sample answer provided at the back of the book.

possession of her [people] land when the god Poseidon wants it. **12**

[Athena and Poseidon] skills are different, and each promises a special

gift to the Athenians. **13** At the [contest] conclusion, Poseidon has

given water and Athena has given an olive tree, for sustenance. **14** The

other gods decide that the [Athenians] lives depend more on Athena

than on Poseidon.

Exercise 42.2   **LBCH 42a**
Revising: Apostrophes with possessives

In the following paragraph, insert or reposition apostrophes as
needed and delete any needless apostrophes. If a sentence is correct as given, mark the number preceding it.

*1 The eastern coast of Belize was once a fishermans paradise, but

overfishing caused the fishing industrys sharp decline in this Central

American country. **2** The country's government is now showing the

world that leaders' foresight can turn a problem into an opportunity.

3 Belize is capitalizing on something that can capture tourists interest:

whale sharks. **4** Huge but harmless to people, whale sharks regularly

*Sample answer provided at the back of the book.

visit Belizes coast to feed on smaller fishes eggs. **5** The predictable gatherings of the shark's attract large numbers of scuba diver's and snorkeler's, so that the fishs' fascinating beauty has become an economic treasure. **6** A tourists eagerness to spend money for an up-close view of whale sharks is Belizes renewable and reliable resource.

Exercise 42.3   LBCH 42b
Distinguishing between plurals and possessives

Supply the appropriate form—possessive or plural—of each word given in brackets. Some words require apostrophes, and some do not.

Example:

A dozen Hawaiian [shirt], each with [it] own loud design, hung in the window.

A dozen Hawaiian shirts, each with its own loud design, hung in the window.

*1 Demeter may be the oldest of the ancient Greek [god], older than Zeus. **2** In myth she is the earth mother, which means that the responsibility for the fertility of both [animal] and [plant] is [she]. **3** Many prehistoric [culture] had earth [goddess] like Demeter. **4** In Greek culture the [goddess] festival came at harvest time, with [it] cel-

*Sample answer provided at the back of the book.

ebration of bounty. **5** The [people] [prayer] to Demeter thanked her for

grain and other [gift].

Exercise 42.4   *LBCH 42b*
Revising: Misuses of the apostrophe

Revise the following paragraph by deleting or repositioning apostrophes or by repairing incorrect possessive pronouns or contractions. If a sentence is correct as given, mark the number preceding it.

*1 Research is proving that athlete's who excel at distance running

have physical characteristics that make them faster than most people.

2 For example, they're hearts are larger. **3** An average adult's heart

pump's about fifteen liters of blood per minute, but a competitive dis-

tance runner's heart circulate's twice as much. **4** Elite runners are also

more efficient: they're able to run with less work than less talented run-

ners must exert. **5** In addition, competitive runner's are able to keep

running for long time's at high levels of exertion. **6** Although these

abilities can be honed in training, they cannot be acquired by a run-

ner: they are his' or her's from birth.

**Sample answer provided at the back of the book.

Exercise 42.5   LBCH 42b
Revising: Contractions and personal pronouns

Revise the following paragraph to correct mistakes in the use of contractions and personal pronouns. If a sentence is correct as given, mark the number preceding it.

*1 Roald Dahl's children's novel *James and the Giant Peach* has

been enjoyed by each generation of readers since its first publication

in 1961. ***2** Its a magical story of adventure and friendship. **3** James, a

lonely boy whose being raised by his two nasty aunts, accidentally

drops some mysterious crystals by an old peach tree in the yard. **4** The

peach at the very top grows to an enormous size, and when James

crawls inside, he finds friendly, oversized bugs ready to welcome him

into there family. **5** As the peach breaks from the tree and rolls into the

ocean, their plunged into an adventure that takes them to the top of

the Empire State Building.

Exercise 42.6 Forming contractions   LBCH 42c

Form contractions from each set of words below. Use each contraction in a complete sentence.

*Sample answer provided at the back of the book.

Example:
we are: we're
<u>We're</u> open to ideas.

*1 she would

2 could not

3 they are

4 he is

5 do not

6 she will

7 hurricane of 1962

8 is not

*Sample answer provided at the back of the book.

9 it is

10 will not

Exercise 42.7   *LBCH 42c*
Revising: Contractions and personal pronouns

Revise the following paragraph to correct mistakes in the use of contractions and personal pronouns. If a sentence is correct as given, mark the number preceding it.

*1 In Greek myth the goddess Demeter has a special fondness for

Eleusis, near Athens, and it's people. 2 She finds rest among the peo-

ple and is touched by their kindness. 3 As a reward Demeter gives the

Eleusians the secret for making they're land fruitful. 4 The Eleusians

begin a cult in honor of Demeter, whose worshiped in secret cere-

monies. 5 Its unknown what happened in the ceremonies, for no par-

ticipant ever revealed there rituals.

*Sample answer provided at the back of the book.

Exercise 42.8 Revising: Apostrophes   LBCH 42

Revise the following paragraph to correct mistakes in the use of apostrophes or any confusion between contractions and possessive personal pronouns. If a sentence is correct as given, mark the number preceding it.

*1 Landlocked Chad is among the worlds most troubled countries.

*2 The people's of Chad are poor: they're average per capita income equals $1000 per year. **3** Less than half of Chads population is literate, and every five hundred people must share only two teacher's. **4** The natural resources of the nation have never been plentiful, and now, as it's slowly being absorbed into the growing Sahara Desert, even water is scarce. **5** Chads political conflicts go back to the nineteenth century, when the French colonized the land by brutally subduing it's people. **6** The rule of the French—who's inept government of the colony did nothing to ease tensions among racial, tribal, and religious group's—ended with independence in 1960. **7** But since then the Chadians experience has been one of civil war and oppression, and their also threatened with invasions from they're neighbors.

Exercise 43.1   LBCH 43a, 43b
Revising: Double and single quotation marks

Insert double and single quotation marks as needed in the following sentences. Mark the number preceding any sentence that is already correct.

*1 Why, the lecturer asked, do we say Bless you! or something else when people sneeze but not acknowledge coughs, hiccups, and other eruptions?

2 She said that sneezes have always been regarded differently.

3 Sneezes feel more uncontrollable than some other eruptions, she said.

4 Unlike coughs and hiccups, she explained, sneezes feel as if they come from inside the head.

5 She concluded, People thus wish to recognize a sneeze, if only with a Gosh.

Exercise 43.2   LBCH 43d
Revising: Quotation marks for titles

Insert quotation marks as needed for titles and words in the following sentences. If quotation marks should be used instead of underlining, insert them.

*1 In Chapter 8, titled How to Be Interesting, the author explains the art of conversation.

2 The Beatles' song Let It Be reminds Martin of his uncle.

3 The article that appeared in <u>Mental Health</u> was titled <u>Children of Divorce Ask, "Why?"</u>

4 In the encyclopedia the discussion under Modern Art fills less than a column.

5 One prizewinning essay, <u>Cowgirls on Wall Street</u>, first appeared in <u>Entrepreneur</u> magazine.

Exercise 43.3 Revising: Quotation marks   LBCH 43f

Some of the underlined words in the following paragraph are direct quotations or should be quoted titles. Remove incorrect underlining, and insert quotation marks. Be sure that other marks of punctuation are correctly placed inside or outside the quotation marks.

*1 In the title essay of her book <u>The Death of the Moth and Other</u>

<u>Essays</u>, Virginia Woolf describes the last moments of a <u>frail and diminu-</u>

<u>tive body</u>. **2** An insect's death may seem insignificant, but the moth is,

in Woolf's words, <u>life, a pure bead</u>. **3** The moth's struggle against

death, <u>indifferent, impersonal</u>, is heroic. **4** Where else but in such a bit

of life could one see a protest so <u>superb</u>? **5** At the end of <u>The Death of</u>

---

*Sample answer provided at the back of the book.

the Moth, Woolf sees the insect lying <u>most decently and uncomplain-</u>

<u>ingly composed</u>; in death it finds dignity.

Exercise 43.4   *LBCH 43*
Revising: Quotation marks

Insert quotation marks as needed in the following paragraph. If a
sentence is correct as given, mark the number preceding it.

*1 In one class we talked about a passage from I Have a Dream,

the speech delivered by Martin Luther King, Jr., on the steps of the

Lincoln Memorial on August 28, 1963:

> **2** When the architects of our republic wrote the magnifi-
>
> cent words of the Constitution and the Declaration of Inde-
>
> pendence, they were signing a promissory note to which
>
> every American was to fall heir. **3** This note was a promise
>
> that all men would be guaranteed the unalienable rights of
>
> life, liberty, and the pursuit of happiness.

4 What did Dr. King mean by this statement? the teacher asked. **5** Per-

haps we should define promissory note first. **6** Then she explained that a person who signs such a note agrees to pay a specific sum of money

on a particular date or on demand by the holder of the note. **7** One

student suggested, Maybe Dr. King meant that the writers of the Con-

stitution and Declaration promised that all people in America should

be equal. **8** He and over 200,000 people had gathered in Washington,

DC, added another student. **9** Maybe their purpose was to demand

payment, to demand those rights for African Americans. **10** The whole

discussion was an eye-opener for those of us (including me) who had

never considered that those documents make promises that we

should expect our country to fulfill.

Exercise 44.1 Revising: Dashes   LBCH 44a
Insert dashes as needed in the following paragraph.

*1 The movie-theater business is undergoing dramatic changes

changes that may affect what movies are made and shown. **2** The clos-

ing of independent theaters, the control of theaters by fewer and

fewer owners, and the increasing ownership of theaters by movie stu-

*Sample answer provided at the back of the book.

dios and distributors these changes may reduce the availability of non-commercial films. **3** Yet at the same time the number of movie screens is increasing primarily in multiscreen complexes so that smaller films may find more outlets. **4** The number of active movie screens that is, screens showing films or booked to do so is higher now than at any time since World War II. **5** The biggest theater complexes seem to be something else as well art galleries, amusement arcades, restaurants, spectacles.

Exercise 44.2 Revising: Parentheses   **LBCH 44b**

Insert parentheses around parenthetical expressions in the following paragraph.

*1 Many of those involved in the movie business agree that multiscreen complexes are good for two reasons: 1 they cut the costs of exhibitors, and 2 they offer more choices to audiences. **2** However, those who produce and distribute films and not just the big studios argue that the multiscreen theaters give exhibitors too much power. **3**

The major studios are buying movie theaters to gain control over important parts of the distribution process what gets shown and for how much money. **4** For twelve years 1938–50 the federal government forced the studios to sell all their movie theaters. **5** But because they now have more competition television and DVD players, for instance, the studios are permitted to own theaters.

Exercise 44.3 Using ellipsis marks   LBCH 44c

Use ellipsis marks and any other needed punctuation to follow the numbered instructions for quoting from the following paragraph.

Women in the sixteenth and seventeenth centuries were educated in the home and, in some cases, in boarding schools. Men were educated at home, in grammar schools, and at the universities. The universities were closed to female students. For women, "learning the Bible," as Elizabeth Joceline puts it, was an impetus to learning to read. To be able to read the Bible in the vernacular was a liberating experience that freed the reader from hearing only the set passages read in the church and interpreted by the church. A Protestant woman was expected to read the scriptures daily, to meditate on them, and to memorize portions of them. In addition, a woman was expected to instruct her entire household in "learning the Bible" by holding instructional and devotional times each day for all household members, including the servants.
                   —Charlotte F. Otten, *English Women's Voices, 1540–1700*

*1 Quote the fifth sentence, but omit everything from *that freed the reader* to the end.

*Sample answer provided at the back of the book.

2 Quote the fifth sentence, but omit the words *was a liberating experience that.*

3 Quote the first and sixth sentences.

Exercise 44.4   *LBCH 44*
Revising: Dashes, parentheses, ellipsis marks, brackets, slashes

Insert dashes, parentheses, ellipsis marks, brackets, or slashes as needed in the following paragraph. In some cases, two or more different marks could be correct.

*1 "Let all the learned say what they can, 'Tis ready money makes

the man." ***2** These two lines of poetry by the Englishman William

Somerville 1645–1742 may apply to a current American economic

problem. **3** Non-American investors with "ready money" pour some of

it as much as $1.3 trillion in recent years into the United States. **4**

Stocks and bonds, savings deposits, service companies, factories, art-

*Sample answer provided at the back of the book.

works, political campaigns the investments of foreigners are varied and

grow more numerous every day. 5 Proponents of foreign investment

argue that it revives industry, strengthens the economy, creates jobs

more than 3 million, they say, and encourages free trade among

nations. 6 Opponents caution that the risks associated with heavy for-

eign investment namely decreased profits at home and increased polit-

ical influence from outside may ultimately weaken the economy. 7 On

both sides, it seems, "the learned say, 'Tis ready money makes the man

or country." 8 The question is, whose money theirs or ours?

PART 6

Spelling and Mechanics

Exercise 45.1   LBCH 45b
Distinguishing between ie and ei

Insert *ie* or *ei* in the words below. Check doubtful spellings in a dictionary.

*1 br____f	7 gr____vance	13 h____ght
*2 dec____ve	8 f____nd	14 fr____ght
3 rec____pt	9 l____surely	15 f____nt
4 s____ze	10 ach____ve	16 s____ve
5 for____gn	11 pat____nce	
6 pr____st	12 p____rce	

Exercise 45.2 Revising: ie and ei   LBCH 45b

In the following paragraph, revise any incorrect spellings of words with *ie* or *ei*. If a sentence is correct as given, mark the number preceding it.

*Sample answer provided at the back of the book.

*1 Many people perceive donating blood as a rewarding experience. *2 Giving blood is niether painful nor wierd, although many people beleive it is both. 3 It takes a leisurely half hour or so, and it gives one a feeling of having acheived something. 4 In truth, there is a slight sting when the needle is inserted into the vien, so the best thing to do then is to focus on something else, like the cieling. 5 After donating blood once, you can expect to receive regular invitations from the blood center to give blood again.

Exercise 45.3   *LBCH 45b*
Keeping or dropping a final e

Combine the following words and endings, keeping or dropping a final *e* as necessary to make correctly spelled words. Check doubtful spellings in a dictionary.

*1 malice + ious   _____

*2 love + able   _____

3 service + able   _____

4 retire + ment   _____

5 sue + ing   _____

6 virtue + ous   _____

7 note + able   _____

8 battle + ing   _____

9 suspense + ion _____

Exercise 45.4 Revising: Final e   *LBCH 45b*

In the following paragraph, revise any incorrect changes in words with a final *e*. If a sentence is correct as given, mark the number preceding it.

*1 For decades scientists have been secureing metal and plastic bands to the flippers of penguins and useing the numbered bands to observe the birds' behavior. 2 Recently, a five-year study produced truely convinceing evidence that the bands themselves are influenceing the penguins' behavior. 3 For instance, banded penguins are less likly to produce offspring. 4 The researchers recommended replacing the bands with tiny electronic devices implanted under the birds' skin.

*Sample answer provided at the back of the book.

Exercise 45.5
Keeping or dropping a final y   *LBCH 45b*

Combine the following words and endings, changing or keeping a final y as necessary to make correctly spelled words. Check doubtful spellings in a dictionary.

*1 imply + s   _____

*2 messy + er   _____

3 apply + ing   _____

4 delay + ing   _____

5 defy + ance   _____

6 say + s   _____

7 solidify + s   _____

8 Murphy + s   _____

9 supply + ed   _____

Exercise 45.6 Revising: Final y   *LBCH 45b*

In the following paragraph, revise any incorrect changes in words with a final y. If a sentence is correct as given, mark the number preceding it.

*Sample answer provided at the back of the book.

*1 My neighbor, Mr. Sorsky, often says he is worryed about his job. 2 However, today's harryed white-collar workers, like Mr. Sorsky, have a much easyer situation than did workers of a hundred years ago. 3 Most men used to work in such industrys as farming, mining, and steelworking, in which job loss and injurys were common. 4 Women often worked in low-paying jobs as domestics or millworkers. 5 Many of today's working poor still labor in such triing situations. 6 Perhaps the middle-class Mr. Sorskies of the world should count their blessings instead of complaining about their troubles.

Exercise 45.7 Doubling consonants   *LBCH 45b*

Combine the following words and endings, doubling final consonants as necessary to make correctly spelled words. Check doubtful spellings in a dictionary.

*1 repair + ing   _____

*2 admit + ance   _____

3 benefit + ed   _____

4 shop + ed   _____

*Sample answer provided at the back of the book.

5 conceal + ed _____

6 allot + ed   _____

7 drip + ing   _____

8 declaim + ed _____

9 parallel + ing _____

Exercise 45.8 Revising: Consonants   LBCH 45b

In the following paragraph, revise any incorrect changes in words ending in consonants. If a sentence is correct as given, mark the number preceding it.

*1 People have always been charmmed by the idea of walking on

water. 2 A new device, the W Boat, finaly allows just that. 3 By pair-

ring two connected, buoyant platforms, the inventor of the W Boat

created something like long, floatting snowshoes for use on water.

4 Fiting the W Boat technology to everyday use, the inventor also

developped a "paddle-skiing" device, which allows a person to pad-

*Sample answer provided at the back of the book.

dle while standing. **5** Now strolling on water, as many have dreamed

of doing, is an actuality.

Exercise 45.9 Attaching prefixes   ***LBCH 45b***

Combine the following prefixes and words to make correctly
spelled words. Check doubtful spellings in a dictionary.

*1 mis + place   _____

*2 self + conscious _____

3 dis + service   _____

4 pre + conception_____

5 anti + American _____

6 un + fold   _____

7 dis + charge   _____

8 mis + shape   _____

9 under + run   _____

*Sample answer provided at the back of the book.

Exercise 45.10 Revising: Prefixes   *LBCH 45b*

In the following paragraph, revise any incorrect spellings of words with prefixes. If a sentence is correct as given, mark the number preceding it.

*1 People often seem to regard bacteria as somehow unatural intruders in human biology. 2 This notion is missinformed, however. 3 Even though it seems ilogical, most bacteria in fact improve health and prolong life. 4 The health benefits of antibacterial soaps and cleaners are overrated. 5 In most situations such products are unecessary to fight disease, and they can kill bacteria we require. 6 The best yet most underated way to kill harmful bacteria is simple, thorough, and frequent handwashing.

Exercise 45.11 Forming plurals   *LBCH 45b*

Make correct plurals of the following singular words. Check doubtful spellings in a dictionary.

*1 pile   _____

*2 donkey   _____

*Sample answer provided at the back of the book.

3 beach   _____

4 summary   _____

5 mile per hour   _____

6 box   _____

7 switch   _____

8 sister-in-law   _____

9 Bales   _____

10 cupful   _____

11 libretto   _____

12 video   _____

13 thief   _____

14 goose   _____

15 hiss   _____

16 appendix   _____

Exercise 45.12 Revising: Plurals   LBCH 45b

In the following paragraph, revise any incorrect spellings of plural nouns.

*1 Fewer original video games are available these dayes, but sales and production of sequeles to popular games are strong. 2 Mainstream game publishers follow formulaes that have proved profitable, and sequeles are cheaper to produce than original games. 3 What's more, many video game enthusiastes tend to buy new versions of games they already know. 4 Many players crave original games and think of publishers as thiefs because they merely trade on previous successs. 5 But publishers have found that trying to be heros by following their hunchs often results in low profits.

Exercise 45.13   LBCH 45b
Using correct spellings

In the following paragraph, select the correct spellings from the choices in brackets. Refer as needed to the list of words and rules in Chapter 45 or to a dictionary.

*1 Science [affects, effects] many [important, importent] aspects

*Sample answer provided at the back of the book.

of our lives, though many people have a [pore, poor] understanding

of the [role, roll] of scientific breakthroughs in [their, they're] health.

2 Many people [beleive, believe] that [docters, doctors], more than sci-

ence, are [responsable, responsible] for [improvements, improvments]

in health care. **3** But scientists in the [labratory, laboratory] have made

crucial steps in the search for [knowlege, knowledge] about health and

[medecine, medicine]. **4** For example, one scientist [who's, whose] dis-

coveries have [affected, effected] many people is Ulf Von Euler. **5** In the

1950s Von Euler's discovery of certain hormones [lead, led] to the

invention of the birth control pill. **6** Von Euler's work was used by John

Rock, who [developed, developped] the first birth control pill and

influenced family [planing, planning]. **7** Von Euler also discovered the

[principal, principle] neurotransmitter that controls the heartbeat.

8 Another scientist, Hans Selye, showed what [affect, effect] stress can

have on the body. **9** His findings have [lead, led] to methods of

[baring, bearing] stress.

Exercise 45.14   *LBCH 45b*
Working with a spelling checker

Try your computer's spelling checker on the following paragraph.
Type the paragraph and run it through your spelling checker. Then
proofread it to correct the errors missed by the checker. (Hint:
There are fourteen errors in all.)

*1 The whether effects all of us, though it's affects are different for

different people. 2 Some people love a fare day with warm tempera-

tures and sunshine. 3 They revel in spending a hole day outside with-

out the threat of rein. 4 Other people prefer dark, rainy daze. 5 They

relish the opportunity to slow down and here they're inner thoughts.

6 Most people agree, however, that to much of one kind of whether—

reign, sun, snow, or clouds—makes them board.

Exercise 45.15   *LBCH 45c*
Using hyphens in compound words

Insert hyphens as needed in the following compounds, consulting a
dictionary as needed. If a compound is correct as given, mark the
number preceding it.

*1 reimburse   _____

*2 deescalate   _____

*Sample answer provided at the back of the book.

3 forty odd soldiers _____

4 little known bar _____

5 seven eighths _____

6 seventy eight _____

7 happy go lucky _____

8 preexisting   _____

9 senator elect   _____

10 postwar   _____

11 two and six person cars _____

12 ex songwriter   _____

13 V shaped   _____

14 reeducate   _____

Exercise 45.16 Revising: Hyphens   LBCH 45c

Insert hyphens as needed in the following paragraph, and delete them where they are not needed. If a sentence is correct as given, mark the number preceding it.

*1 The African elephant is well known for its size. *2 A male elephant weighs five and one half to six tons, and a female weighs up to four tons. 3 Even with the difference in weight, both male and female elephants can grow to a ten-foot height. 4 A newborn elephant calf weighs two to three hundred pounds and stands about thirty three inches high. 5 A two hundred pound, thirty three inch baby is quite a big baby! 6 African elephants reach maturity at the age of fourteen or fifteen and often live for sixty five or seventy years.

Exercise 46.1 Revising: Capitals   LBCH 46

Revise the following paragraph to correct errors in capitalization, consulting a dictionary as needed. If a sentence is correct as given, mark the number preceding it.

*1 San Antonio, texas, is a thriving city in the southwest that has always offered much to tourists interested in the roots of spanish set-

*Sample answer provided at the back of the book.

tlement in the new world. *2 Most visitors stop at the Alamo, one of five Catholic Missions built by Priests to convert native americans and to maintain spain's claims in the area. 3 The Alamo is famous for being the site of an 1836 battle that helped to create the republic of Texas. 4 San Antonio has grown tremendously in recent years. 5 The Hemisfair plaza and the San Antonio river link tourist and convention facilities. 6 Restaurants, Hotels, and shops line the River. 7 the haunting melodies of "Una paloma blanca" and "malagueña" lure passing tourists into Casa rio and other mexican restaurants. 8 The university of Texas at San Antonio has expanded, and a Medical Center lies in the Northwest part of the city. 9 Sea World, on the west side of San Antonio, entertains grandparents, fathers and mothers, and children with the antics of dolphins and seals. 10 The City has attracted high-tech industry, creating a corridor between san antonio and austin.

*Sample answer provided at the back of the book.

Exercise 47.1   *LBCH 47*
Revising: Underlining or italics

Underline or italicize words and phrases as needed in the following paragraph, or delete the underlining from any words or phrases that are highlighted unnecessarily. If a sentence is correct as given, mark the number preceding it.

*1 A number of veterans of the war in Vietnam have become prominent writers. *2 Oliver Stone is perhaps the most famous for writing and directing the films Platoon and Born on the Fourth of July.

3 The fiction writer Tim O'Brien has published short stories about the war in Esquire, GQ, and Massachusetts Review. 4 His dreamlike novel Going After Cacciato is about the horrors of combat. 5 Typically for veterans' writing, the novel uses words and phrases borrowed from Vietnamese, such as di di mau ("go quickly") or dinky dau ("crazy").

6 Another writer, Philip Caputo, provides a gripping account of his service in Vietnam in the book A Rumor of War. 7 Caputo's book was made into a television movie, also titled A Rumor of War. 8 The playwright David Rabe—in such dramas as The Basic Training of Pavlo Hummel,

Streamers, and Sticks and Bones—depicts the effects of war not only

on the soldiers but on their families. **9** Steve Mason, called the poet

laureate of the Vietnam war, has published two collections of poems

on the war: Johnny's Song and Warrior for Peace. **10** And Rod Kane

wrote an autobiography about the war, Veterans Day, that received

rave reviews in the Washington Post.

Exercise 48.1 Revising: Abbreviations   LBCH 48

Revise the following paragraph as needed to correct inappropriate use of abbreviations for nontechnical writing. If a sentence is correct as given, mark the number preceding it.

*1 In an issue of *Science* magazine, Dr. Virgil L. Sharpton discusses

a theory that could help explain the extinction of dinosaurs. ***2**

According to the theory, a comet or asteroid crashed into the earth

about 65 mill. yrs. ago. **3** The result was a huge crater about 10 km.

(6.2 mi.) deep in the Gulf of Mex. **4** Sharpton's measurements suggest

that the crater is 50 pct. larger than scientists had previously believed.

5 Indeed, 20-yr.-old drilling cores reveal that the crater is about 186

---

*Sample answer provided at the back of the book.

mi. wide, roughly the size of Conn. **6** The space object was traveling

more than 100,000 miles per hour and hit earth with the impact of

100 to 300 megatons of TNT. **7** On impact, 200,000 cubic km. of rock

and soil were vaporized or thrown into the air. **8** That's the equivalent

of 2.34 bill. cubic ft. of matter. **9** The impact would have created 400-

ft. tidal waves across the Atl. Ocean, temps. higher than 20,000 degs.,

and powerful earthquakes. **10** Sharpton theorizes that the dust, vapor,

and smoke from this impact blocked the sun's rays for mos., cooled

the earth, and thus resulted in the death of the dinosaurs.

Exercise 49.1 Revising: Numbers   **LBCH 49**

Revise the following paragraphs so that numbers are used appropriately for nontechnical writing. If a sentence is correct as given, mark the number preceding it.

*1 The planet Saturn is nine hundred million miles, or nearly one

billion five hundred million kilometers, from the sun. **2** Saturn orbits

the sun only two and four-tenths times during the average human life

span. **3** As a result, a year on Saturn equals almost thirty of our years.

*Sample answer provided at the back of the book.

4 The planet travels in its orbit at about twenty-one thousand six hundred miles per hour.

5 Saturn is huge: more than seventy-two thousand miles in diameter, compared to Earth's eight-thousand-mile diameter. **6** Saturn is also very cold, with an average temperature of minus two hundred and eighteen degrees Fahrenheit, compared to Earth's fifty-nine degrees Fahrenheit. **7** Saturn is cold because of its great distance from the sun and because its famous rings reflect almost 70 percent of the sunlight that approaches the planet. **8** The ring system is almost forty thousand miles wide, beginning 8800 miles from the planet's visible surface and ending forty-seven thousand miles from that surface.

PART 7

Research Writing

Exercise 52.1 Synthesizing sources   *LBCH 52b*

The three passages below address the same issue, the legalization of drugs. What similarities do you see in the authors' ideas? What differences? Write a paragraph of your own in which you use these authors' views as a point of departure for your own view about drug legalization. (A sample analysis of the similarities and differences appears at the end of this book.)

Perhaps the most unfortunate victims of drug prohibition laws have been the residents of America's ghettos. These laws have proved largely futile in deterring ghetto-dwellers from becoming drug abusers, but they do account for much of what ghetto residents identify as the drug problem. Aggressive, gun-toting drug dealers often upset law-abiding residents far more than do addicts nodding out in doorways. Meanwhile other residents perceive the drug dealers as heroes and successful role models. They're symbols of success to children who see no other options. At the same time the increasingly harsh criminal penalties imposed on adult drug dealers have led drug traffickers to recruit juveniles. Where once children started dealing drugs only after they had been using them for a few years, today the sequence is often reversed. Many children start using drugs only after working for older drug dealers for a while. Legalization of drugs, like legalization of alcohol in the 1930s, would drive the drug-dealing business off the streets and out of apartment buildings and into government-regulated, tax-paying stores. It also would force many of the gun-toting dealers out of the business and convert others into legitimate businessmen.

—Ethan A. Nadelmann, "Shooting Up"

Statistics argue against legalization. The University of Michigan conducts an annual survey of twelfth graders, asking the students about their drug consumption. In 1980, 56.4 percent of those polled said they had used marijuana in the past twelve months, whereas in 2004 only 45.7 percent had done so. Cocaine use was also reduced in the same period (22.6 percent to 15.4 percent). At the same time, twelve-month use of legally available drugs—alcohol and nicotine-containing cigarettes—remained constant at about 75 percent and 55 percent, respectively. The numbers of illegal drug users haven't declined nearly enough: those teenaged marijuana and cocaine users are still vulnerable to addiction and even death, and they threaten to infect their impressionable peers. But clearly the prohibition of illegal drugs has helped, while the legal status of alcohol and cigarettes has not made them less popular.

—Sylvia Runkle, "The Case Against Legalization"

I have to laugh at the debate over what to do about the drug problem. Everyone is running around offering solutions—from making drug use a more serious criminal offense to legalizing it. But there isn't a real solution. I know that. I used and abused drugs, and people, and society, for two decades. Nothing worked to get me to stop all that behavior except just plain being sick and tired. Nothing. Not threats, not ten-plus years in prison, not anything that was said to me. I used until I got through. Period. And that's when you'll win the war. When all the dope fiends are done. Not a minute before.

—Michael W. Posey, "I Did Drugs Until
They Wore Me Out. Then I Stopped."

Similarities:

Differences:

Paragraph:

Exercise 52.2   *LBCH 52d*
Summarizing and paraphrasing

Prepare two source notes, one summarizing the entire paragraph
below and the other paraphrasing the first four sentences (ending
with the word *autonomy*). Use the format for a note illustrated in
Chapter 52, omitting only the subject heading. (A sample summary
appears at the end of the book.)

Federal organization [of the United States] has made it possible for
the different states to deal with the same problems in many different
ways. One consequence of federalism, then, has been that people are
treated differently, by law, from state to state. The great strength of
this system is that differences from state to state in cultural prefer-
ences, moral standards, and levels of wealth can be accommodated. In
contrast to a unitary system in which the central government makes all
important decisions (as in France), federalism is a powerful arrangement for maximizing regional freedom and autonomy. The great
weakness of our federal system, however, is that people in some states
receive less than the best or the most advanced or the least expensive
services and policies that government can offer. The federal dilemma

does not invite easy solution, for the costs and benefits of the arrangement have tended to balance out.

—Peter K. Eisinger et al., *American Politics*, p. 44

Summary:

Paraphrase of first four sentences:

Exercise 52.3   **LBCH 52d**
Combining summary, paraphrase,
and direct quotation

Prepare a source note containing a combination of paraphrase or summary and direct quotation that states the main idea of the passage below. Use the format for a note illustrated in Chapter 52, omitting only the subject heading.

*Most speakers unconsciously duel even during seemingly casual conversations, as can often be observed at social gatherings where they show less concern for exchanging information with other guests than for asserting their own dominance. Their verbal dueling often employs very subtle weapons like mumbling, a hostile act which defeats the listener's desire to understand what the speaker claims he is trying to say (but is really not saying because he is mumbling!). Or the verbal dueler may keep talking after someone has passed out of hearing range—which is often an aggressive challenge to the listener to return and acknowledge the dominance of the speaker.

—Peter K. Farb, *Word Play*, p. 107

Statement of main idea (quotation and summary or paraphrase):

Exercise 52.4   LBCH 52e
Introducing and interpreting borrowed material

Drawing on the ideas in the following paragraph and using examples from your own observations and experiences, write a paragraph about anxiety. Integrate at least one direct quotation and one paraphrase from the following paragraph into your own sentences. In your paragraph identify the author by name and give his credentials:

*Sample answer provided at the back of the book.

he is a professor of psychiatry and a practicing psychoanalyst. (A sample beginning for a paragraph appears at the end of the book.)

There are so many ways in which human beings are different from all the lower forms of animals, and almost all of them make us uniquely susceptible to feelings of anxiousness. Our imagination and reasoning powers facilitate anxiety; the anxious feeling is precipitated not by an absolute impending threat—such as the worry about an examination, a speech, travel—but rather by the symbolic and often unconscious representations. We do not have to be experiencing a potential danger. We can experience something related to it. We can recall, through our incredible memories, the original symbolic sense of vulnerability in childhood and suffer the feeling attached to that. We can even forget the original memory and be stuck with the emotion—which is then compounded by its seemingly irrational quality at this time. It is not just the fear of death which pains us, but the anticipation of it; or the anniversary of a specific death; or a street, a hospital, a time of day, a color, a flower, a symbol associated with death.
—Willard Gaylin, "Feeling Anxious," p. 23

Paragraph:

Exercise 53.1
Recognizing plagiarism

LBCH 53c

The following numbered items show various attempts to quote or paraphrase the passage below. Carefully compare each attempt with the original passage. Which attempts are plagiarized, inaccurate, or both, and which are acceptable? Why?

I would agree with the sociologists that psychiatric labeling is dangerous. Society can inflict terrible wounds by discrimination, and by confusing health with disease and disease with badness.
    —George E. Vaillant, *Adaptation to Life*, p. 361

*1 According to George Vaillant, society often inflicts wounds by using psychiatric labeling, confusing health, disease, and badness (361).

2 According to George Vaillant, "psychiatric labeling [such as 'homosexual' or 'schizophrenic'] is dangerous. Society can inflict terrible wounds by . . . confusing health with disease and disease with badness" (361).

3 According to George Vaillant, when psychiatric labeling discriminates between health and disease or between disease and badness, it can inflict wounds on those labeled (361).

*Sample answer provided at the back of the book.

4 Psychiatric labels can badly hurt those labeled, says George Vaillant, because they fail to distinguish among health, illness, and immorality (361).

5 Labels such as "homosexual" and "schizophrenic" can be hurtful when they fail to distinguish among health, illness, and immorality.

6 "I would agree with the sociologists that society can inflict terrible wounds by discrimination, and by confusing health with disease and disease with badness" (Vaillant 361).

PART 8

Writing in the Disciplines

Exercise 58.1   *LBCH 58b*
Writing works-cited entries

Prepare works-cited entries from the following information. Follow the models of the *MLA Handbook* given in Chapter 58 unless your instructor specifies a different style. For titles, use underlining (as here) unless your instructor requests italics. Arrange the finished entries in alphabetical order, not numbered.

*1 A journal article titled "Networking the Classroom" by Christopher Conte. The article appears in volume 5 of <u>CQ Researcher</u>, a journal that pages issues continuously throughout each annual volume. Volume 5 is dated 2004. The article runs from page 923 to page 943.

2 A magazine article on a database that is also available in print. The author is Larry Irving. The title is "The Still Yawning Divide." The article appears in the March 12, 2005, issue of <u>Newsweek</u>, a weekly magazine, and starts on page 64. You consulted the article on November 14, 2005, through the database <u>Expanded Academic ASAP</u> from the service InfoTrac (http://www.galegroup.com). You reached the database through Southeast State University's Polk Library.

*Sample answer provided at the back of the book.

3 A government document you consulted on November 12, 2005, over the Internet. The author is the National Center for Education Statistics, an agency within the United States Department of Education. The title of the document is Internet Access in Public Schools. It was published February 24, 2005, and can be accessed at http://www.ed.gov/nces/edstats.

4 A book called Failure to Connect: How Computers Affect Our Children's Minds—For Better and Worse, written by Jane M. Healy and published in 2000 by Simon & Schuster in New York.

5 An article in the October 9, 2004, issue of the magazine The Nation titled "The Threat to the Net." The article is by Jeff Chester and appears on pages 6 to 7 of the magazine. You found it through Polk Library at Southeast State University on November 14, 2005, using the database Expanded Academic ASAP from the service InfoTrac. The home page URL for the database is http://www.galegroup.com.

6 A pamphlet titled Bridging the Digital Divide, with no named author. It was published in 2005 by the ALA in Chicago.

7 An article titled "MyPyramid.gov: Achieving E-Health for All?" on the Web site Digital Divide Network, sponsored by the Benton Foundation at http://www.digitaldivide.net/articles. The article is by Andy Carvin and is dated February 22, 2005. You found it on November 10, 2005.

8 An e-mail interview you conducted with Mary McArthur on October 31, 2005.

Sample Answers

Exercise 3.1
Evaluating thesis statements, p. 1

1 The statement lacks unity because the two halves do not seem to relate to each other.
   Possible revision: We should channel our natural feelings of aggression toward constructive rather than destructive ends.

2 The statement needs to be more specific: Why is Islam misunderstood in the United States?
   Possible revision: The religion of Islam is widely misunderstood in the United States because many Americans equate televised depictions of Muslim fundamentalists with the religion itself.

Exercise 3.2
Organizing ideas, p. 2

I. Fans resist [new general idea].
   A. Sports seasons are already too crowded for fans.
      1. Baseball, football, hockey, and basketball seasons already overlap.
      2. Fans have limited time to watch.
      3. Fans have limited money to pay for sports.
   B. Soccer is unfamiliar [new general idea].
      1. A lot of kids play soccer in school, but the game is still "foreign."
      2. Soccer rules are unfamiliar.

Exercise 8.1
Using academic language, p. 5

The stereotype that women talk more on cell phones than men do turns out to be false.

Exercise 11.1
Testing argument subjects, p. 6

1 Appropriate for argument, because people can and do disagree based on evidence.
2 Inappropriate for argument: matter of facts, and few people would disagree.

Exercise 11.2
Identifying and revising fallacies, p. 7

1 Begged question.
  A *revision:* The fact that individuals in the United States cannot legally sell nuclear technology to nonnuclear nations, while the government can, points up a disturbing limit on individual rights.

Exercise 15.1
Revising: Emphasis of subjects and verbs, p. 9

1 Many heroes helped to emancipate the slaves.
2 However, Harriet Tubman, an escaped slave herself, stands above the rest.

Exercise 15.2
Sentence combining: Beginnings and endings, p. 10

1 Pat Taylor strode into the packed room, greeting students called "Taylor's Kids" and nodding to their parents and teachers.

2 This wealthy Louisiana oilman had promised his "Kids" free
   college educations because he was determined to make higher
   education available to all qualified but disadvantaged students.

Exercise 15.3
Sentence combining: Coordination, p. 11

1 Many chronic misspellers do not have the time or motivation
   to master spelling rules. They may rely on dictionaries to
   catch misspellings, but most dictionaries list words under
   their correct spellings. One kind of dictionary is designed for
   chronic misspellers. It lists each word under its common *mis*-
   spellings and then provides the correct spelling and definition.

Exercise 15.4
Revising: Subordination for emphasis, p. 12

1 Because soldiers in the Civil War admired their commanding
   officers, they often gave them nicknames containing the word
   old, even though not all of the commanders were old.
2 Confederate General Thomas "Stonewall" Jackson was also
   called "Old Jack," although he was not yet forty years old.

Exercise 15.5
Sentence combining: Subordination, p. 13

1 When the bombardier beetle sees an enemy, it shoots out a jet
   of chemicals to protect itself.
   Seeing an enemy, the bombardier beetle shoots out a jet of
   chemicals to protect itself.

Exercise 15.6
Revising: Effective subordination, p. 14

1 Genaro González is a successful writer whose stories and novels
   have been published to critical acclaim. . . .

Exercise 15.7
Revising: Coordination and subordination, p. 15

Sir Walter Raleigh personified the Elizabethan <u>Age, the</u> period of Elizabeth I's rule of <u>England, in</u> the last half of the sixteenth century.

Exercise 16.1
Revising: Parallelism, p. 17

1 The ancient Greeks celebrated four athletic contests: the Olympic Games at Olympia, the Isthmian <u>Games near</u> Corinth, the <u>Pythian Games at Delphi</u>, and the Nemean Games <u>at Cleonae.</u>

Exercise 16.2
Sentence combining: Parallelism, p. 18

1 People can develop post-traumatic stress disorder (PTSD) after experiencing a dangerous situation and fearing for their survival.

Exercise 17.1
Revising: Variety, p. 19

<u>After being</u> dormant for many years, the Italian volcano Vesuvius exploded on August 24 in the year A<u>D</u> 79.

Exercise 18.1
Revising: Appropriate words, p. 20

1 Acquired immune deficiency syndrome (AIDS) is a <u>serious threat</u> all over the world, and those who think the disease is <u>limited</u> to <u>homosexuals, drug users, and people in other countries</u> are quite mistaken.

2 Indeed, <u>statistics</u> suggest that in the United States one in every five hundred American college <u>students</u> carries the HIV virus that causes AIDS.

3 If such numbers are <u>accurate</u>, then doctors and public health officials will continue to have <u>many</u> HIV and AIDS <u>patients to care for</u> in the years to come.

Exercise 18.2
Revising: Sexist language, p. 22

1 When <u>students apply</u> for <u>jobs</u>, <u>they</u> should prepare the best possible <u>résumés</u>, because the <u>business executives</u> who are scanning <u>stacks</u> of résumés will <u>read them all</u> quickly.

2 <u>Applicants who want their résumés</u> to stand out will make sure <u>they highlight their</u> best points.

Exercise 18.4
Revising: Denotation, p. 25

1 The acclaimed writer Maxine Hong Kingston <u>cites</u> her mother's stories about ancestors and ancient <u>Chinese</u> customs as the sources of her first two books, *The Woman Warrior* and *China Men*.

Exercise 18.5
Considering the connotation of words, p. 26

1 Infection with the AIDS virus, HIV, is a serious health <u>problem</u>.

Exercise 18.6
Revising: Concrete and specific words, p. 27

1 I remember <u>as if it were last week</u> how <u>frightened</u> I felt the first time I <u>crossed the threshold</u> of Mrs. Murphy's second-grade class.

Exercise 18.7
Using concrete and specific words, p. 27

1   fabric, upholstery fabric, velvet
    She chose a wine-colored velvet for backing the pillow.

2   delicious, tart, lemony
    He made a meringue pie, lemony and delicately brown.

Exercise 18.8
Using prepositions in idioms, p. 30

1   The friend who introduced Nick and Lana was proud of his
    matchmaking.
2   They had fallen in love on their first date.

Exercise 18.9
Using prepositions in idioms, p. 31

1   The Eighteenth Amendment to the US Constitution was rati-
    fied in 1919.

Exercise 18.10
Using figurative language, p. 32

1   As the kindergarten children began work on their art projects,
    their voices filled the classroom like water rushing over stones
    in a shallow stream fills the silence of the forest.

Exercise 18.11
Revising: Trite expressions, p. 32

1   The disasters of the war have shaken the small nation severely.

Exercise 19.1
Revising: Completeness, p. 33

1   The first ice cream, eaten in China in about 2000 BC, was
    lumpier than modern ice cream.

Exercise 20.1
Revising: Writing concisely, p. 34

If sore muscles after exercising are a problem for you, there are some <u>things you can do</u> to ease the discomfort.

Exercise 20.2
Revising: Conciseness, p. 35

<u>After much thought</u>, he <u>concluded</u> that carcinogens <u>could be treated like automobiles</u>.

Exercise 21.1
Identifying nouns, pronouns, and verbs, p. 37

        N V   N   P V   N
1 The gingko <u>tree</u> <u>has</u> another <u>name</u>: <u>it</u> <u>is</u> the maidenhair <u>tree</u>.

       N   V   N   N
2 Gingko <u>trees</u> sometimes <u>grow</u> to over a hundred <u>feet</u> in <u>height</u>.

Exercise 21.2
Identifying adjectives and adverbs, p. 38

                             ADJ ADJ   ADJ
1 You can reduce stress by making <u>a</u> <u>few</u> <u>simple</u> changes.

    ADV ADJ   ADV   ADV
2 Get <u>up</u> <u>fifteen</u> minutes <u>earlier</u> than you <u>ordinarily</u> do.

Exercise 21.3
Adding connecting words, p. 39

1 Just about everyone has heard the story <u>of</u> the Trojan Horse.
2 This incident happened at the city of Troy <u>and</u> was planned by the Greeks.

Exercise 22.1
Identifying subjects and predicates, p. 40

> SUBJECT | PREDICATE
> 1 The leaves | fell.
> *Sample imitation:* The kite soared.

Exercise 22.2
Identifying subjects and predicates, p. 41

1 The <u>horse</u> | <u>has</u> a long history of serving humanity but today <u>is</u> mainly a show and sport animal.
2 A member of the genus *Equus*, the domestic <u>horse</u> | <u>is related</u> to the wild Przewalski's horse, the ass, and the zebra.

Exercise 22.3
Identifying sentence parts, p. 42

>   S   V
> 1 The <u>number</u> of serious crimes in the United States <u>decreased</u>.
>   S   V
> 2 A <u>decline</u> in serious crimes <u>occurred</u> each year.

Exercise 22.4
Identifying sentence patterns, p. 43

1 *Find* is transitive.
>   DO   OC
> Many people find <u>New York</u> <u>exciting</u>.

Exercise 23.1
Identifying prepositional phrases, p. 44

>   ┌──── ADVERB ────┐ ┌──── ADVERB ────────┐
> 1 On July 3, 1863, at Gettysburg, Pennsylvania, Robert E. Lee
>   ┌────── ADVERB ──────┐
> gambled unsuccessfully for a Confederate victory in the
> ┌──── ADJECTIVE ────┐
> American Civil War.

2   Called Pickett's Charge, the battle was one of the most
    — ADJECTIVE ——ⲎⲎＡＤＪＥＣＴＩＶＥ ⌐
    disastrous conflicts of the war.

Exercise 23.2
Sentence combining: Prepositional phrases, p. 45

1   The slow loris of Southeast Asia protects itself well with a poi-
    sonous chemical.

Exercise 23.3
Identifying verbals and verbal phrases, p. 46

1   <u>Written in 1850 by Nathaniel Hawthorne</u>, *The Scarlet Letter*
    tells the story of Hester Prynne.

Exercise 23.4
Sentence combining: Verbals and verbal phrases, p. 47

1   Air pollution is a health problem <u>affecting millions of
    Americans</u>.

Exercise 23.5
Sentence combining: Absolute phrases, p. 48

1   <u>Her face beaming</u>, Geraldine Ferraro enjoyed the crowd's
    cheers after her nomination for Vice President.

Exercise 23.6
Sentence combining: Appositive phrases, p. 49

1   Some people, <u>geniuses from birth</u>, perform amazing feats
    when they are very young.

Exercise 23.7
Identifying phrases, p. 50

```
                                    ┌───── appositive phrase ─────┐
          ┌───── prepositional phrase ─────┐        ┌─ prepositional phrase ─┐
1  Because of its many synonyms, or words with similar meanings,
                      ┌───── participial phrase ─────┐
   English can make choosing the right word a difficult task.
   ┌───────────────── participial phrase ─────────────────┐
                                                            prepositional
          ┌───── prepositional phrase ─────┐              ┌─ phrase ─┐
2  Borrowing words from early Germanic languages and from Latin,
                                      prepositional
                                    ┌─ phrase ─┐
   English acquired an unusual number of synonyms.
```

Exercise 23.8
Identifying clauses, p. 51

1 The Prophet Muhammad, <u>who was the founder of Islam</u>, was
   born about 570 CE in the city of Mecca.
   [ADJ]

2 He grew up in the care of his grandfather and an uncle <u>because</u>
   <u>both of his parents had died</u> <u>when he was very young</u>.
   [ADV]   [ADV]

Exercise 23.9
Sentence combining: Subordinate clauses, p. 52

1 Moviegoers expect <u>that</u> movie sequels should be as exciting as
   the original films.

Exercise 24.1
Identifying sentence structures, p. 53

```
         ┌───── MAIN CLAUSE ─────┐        ┌───── MAIN CLAUSE ─────┐
1  Our world has many sounds, but they all have one thing in
   common. [Compound.]
         ┌───────── MAIN CLAUSE ─────────┐
2  They are all produced by vibrations. [Simple.]
```

Exercise 25.1
Using irregular verbs, p. 54

1 The world population had <u>grown</u> by two-thirds of a billion people in less than a decade. [Past participle.]
2 Recently it <u>broke</u> the 6 billion mark. [Past tense.]

Exercise 25.2
Distinguishing between sit/set, lie/lay, rise/raise, p. 56

1 Yesterday afternoon the child <u>lay</u> down for a nap.

Exercise 25.3
Using -s and -ed verb endings, p. 57

1 A teacher sometimes <u>asks</u> too much of a student.
2 In high school I was once <u>punished</u> for being sick.

Exercise 25.4
Using helping verbs, p. 58

1 Each year thousands of new readers <u>have</u> been discovering Agatha Christie's mysteries.

Exercise 25.5
Revising: Helping verbs plus main verbs, p. 58

1 A report from the Bureau of the Census has <u>confirmed</u> a widening gap between rich and poor.

Exercise 25.6
Revising: Verbs plus gerunds or infinitives, p. 59

1 Without enough highly trained people to draw on, American businesses risk <u>losing</u> their competitive edge.

Exercise 25.7
Revising: Verbs plus particles, p. 60

1   American movies treat everything from going out with [correct] someone to making up [correct] an ethnic identity.

Exercise 26.1
Revising: Consistent past tense, p. 61

1   The 1960 presidential race between Richard Nixon and John F. Kennedy was the first to feature a televised debate. [Sentence correct.]
2   Despite his extensive political experience, Nixon <u>perspired</u> heavily and <u>looked</u> haggard and uneasy in front of the camera.

Exercise 26.2
Revising: Consistent present tense, p. 61

1   E. B. White's famous children's novel *Charlotte's Web* is a wonderful story of friendship and loyalty. [Sentence correct.]
2   Charlotte, the wise and motherly spider, <u>decides</u> to save her friend Wilbur, the young and childlike pig, from being butchered by his owner.

Exercise 26.3
Using correct tense sequence, p. 62

1   Diaries that Adolph Hitler <u>was supposed</u> to have written surfaced in Germany.

Exercise 26.4
Revising: Tense sequence with conditional sentences, p. 63

1   If you think you <u>might be</u> exposed to the flu, you should get a flu shot.

Exercise 27.1
Revising: Subjunctive mood, p. 63

1 If John Hawkins <u>had known</u> of all the dangerous side effects of smoking tobacco, <u>would</u> he have introduced the plant to England in 1565?

2 In promoting tobacco, Hawkins noted that if a Florida Indian man <u>were</u> to travel for several days, he <u>would smoke</u> tobacco to satisfy his hunger and thirst.

Exercise 28.1
Converting between active and passive voices, p. 64

1 When <u>engineers</u> <u>built</u> the Eiffel Tower in 1889, the <u>French</u> <u>thought</u> it to be ugly.

Exercise 28.2
Revising: Using the active voice, p. 65

1 Many <u>factors</u> <u>determine</u> water quality.

2 All natural <u>waters</u> <u>contain</u> suspended and dissolved substances.

Exercise 29.1
Revising: Subject-verb agreement, p. 66

1 Statistics from recent research <u>suggest</u> that humor in the workplace relieves job-related stress.

2 Reduced stress in the workplace in turn <u>reduces</u> illness and absenteeism.

3 It can also ease friction within an employee group, which then <u>works</u> together more productively.

Exercise 29.2
Adjusting for subject-verb agreement, p. 68

1 The Siberian <u>tiger</u> <u>is</u> the largest living <u>cat</u> in the world, much bigger than <u>its</u> relative the Bengal tiger.

2 It <u>grows</u> to a length of nine to twelve feet, including <u>its</u> <u>tail</u>, and to a height of about three and a half feet.

3 <u>It</u> can weigh over six hundred pounds.

Exercise 30.1
Choosing between subjective and objective pronouns, p. 69

1 Jody and <u>I</u> had been hunting for jobs.

Exercise 30.2
Choosing between who and whom, p. 70

1 The school administrators suspended Jurgen, <u>whom</u> they suspected of setting the fire.

Exercise 30.3
Sentence combining: Who versus whom, p. 71

1 Some children <u>who</u> have undetected hearing problems may do poorly in school.

Exercise 30.4
Choosing between subjective and objective pronouns, p. 72

1 Obtaining enough protein is important to <u>us</u> vegetarians.

Exercise 30.5
Revising: Pronoun case, p. 72

1 Written four thousand years ago, *The Epic of Gilgamesh* tells of the friendship of Gilgamesh and Enkidu. [Sentence correct.]

2 Gilgamesh was a bored king who his people thought was too harsh. [Sentence correct.]

3 Then he met Enkidu, a wild man <u>who</u> had lived with the animals in the mountains.

Exercise 31.1
Revising: Pronoun-antecedent agreement, p. 74

1   Each girl raised in a Mexican American family in the Rio Grande Valley of Texas hopes that one day <u>she</u> will be given a *quinceañera* party for <u>her</u> fifteenth birthday.
2   Such <u>a celebration is</u> very expensive because it entails a religious <u>service followed</u> by a huge party. *Or:* Such celebrations are very expensive because <u>they entail</u> a religious service followed by a huge party.

Exercise 31.2
Revising: Pronoun-antecedent agreement, p. 75

1   Despite their extensive research and experience, neither child psychologists nor parents have yet figured out how children become who they are. [Sentence correct.]
2   Of course, the family has a tremendous influence on the development of a child in <u>its</u> midst.

Exercise 32.1
Revising: Pronoun reference, p. 76

1   There is a difference between the heroes of modern times and the heroes of earlier times: <u>modern-day heroes</u> have flaws in their characters.

Exercise 32.2
Revising: Pronoun reference, p. 77

1   In Charlotte Brontë's *Jane Eyre*, <u>Jane</u> is a shy young woman who takes a job as a governess.

Exercise 32.3
Revising: Consistency in pronouns, p. 77

1   When <u>taxpayers are</u> waiting to receive <u>tax refunds</u> from the Internal Revenue Service, <u>they</u> begin to notice what time the

mail carrier arrives. *Or:* When <u>you are</u> waiting to receive a tax refund from the Internal Revenue Service, you begin to notice what time the mail carrier arrives.

Exercise 32.4
Revising: Pronoun reference, p. 78

1   "Life begins at forty" is a cliché many people live by, and this <u>saying</u> may or may not be true.

Exercise 33.1
Revising: Adjectives and adverbs, p. 79

1   The eighteenth-century essayist Samuel Johnson fared <u>badly</u> in his early life.

Exercise 33.2
Using comparatives and superlatives, p. 80

1   badly, worse, worst

The favored horse performed <u>badly</u> in the race. He performed <u>worse</u> than all but one other horse. The horse that performed <u>worst</u> broke stride and left the race.

Exercise 33.3
Revising: Comparisons, p. 81

1   The Brontë sisters—Charlotte, Emily, and Anne—are among the <u>most</u> interesting literary families in English history.

Exercise 33.4
Revising: Double negatives, p. 82

1   Interest in books about the founding of the United States is <u>not</u> [*or* <u>hardly</u>] consistent among Americans: it seems to vary with the national mood.

Exercise 33.5
Revising: Present and past participles, p. 83

1 Many critics found Alice Walker's novel *The Color Purple* to be a <u>fascinating</u> book, though the reviews were mixed.
2 One otherwise excited critic wished that Walker had deleted the scenes set in Africa. [Sentence correct.]

Exercise 33.6
Revising: A, an, *and* the, p. 84

1 A recent court case has moved some Native Americans to observe that a lot of people want to be␣Native Americans now that the tribes have something of␣value—namely, gambling casinos.
2 A man named Stephen Jones claimed to be␣Native American in order to open ␣a casino in␣New York's Catskills region.

Exercise 33.7
Revising: Determiners, p. 85

1 <u>Many</u> people love to swim for exercise or just plain fun.

Exercise 33.8
Revising: Adjectives and adverbs, p. 86

1 Americans often argue about which professional sport is <u>best</u>: basketball, football, or baseball.
2 Basketball fans contend that their sport offers more action because the players are <u>constantly</u> running and shooting.

Exercise 34.1
Revising: Misplaced modifiers, p. 87

1 People <u>who are right-handed</u> dominate in our society.

Exercise 34.2
Revising: Misplaced modifiers, p. 87

1 Women have contributed much of significance to American culture.

Exercise 34.3
Arranging adjectives, p. 88

1 Several university researchers are studying image controls for computer graphics.

Exercise 34.4
Revising: Dangling modifiers, p. 90

1 Andrew Jackson's career was legendary in his day. [Sentence correct.]
2 Starting with the American Revolution, Jackson chose service as a mounted courier.

Exercise 34.5
Revising: Misplaced and dangling modifiers, p. 91

1 Several nights a week, Central American tungara frogs silence their mating croaks.

Exercise 35.1
Identifying and revising sentence fragments, p. 91

1 Lacks a subject and a verb.
Complete: A magazine article about vandalism against works of art was interesting.
Combined: In an interesting article about vandalism against works of art, the author says the vandals' motives vary widely.

Exercise 35.2
Revising: Sentence fragments, p. 92

1   Human beings who perfume themselves are not much different from other animals.
2   Animals as varied as insects and dogs release pheromones, chemicals that signal other animals.

Exercise 35.3
Revising: Sentence fragments, p. 94

Baby red-eared slider turtles are brightly colored, with bold patterns on their yellowish undershells that serve as a warning to predators.

Exercise 36.1
Identifying and revising comma splices, p. 95

1   Money has a long history. It goes back at least as far as the earliest records.
    Money has a long history that goes back at least as far as the earliest records.

Exercise 36.2
Identifying and revising fused sentences, p. 96

1   Throughout history money and religion were closely linked; there was little distinction between government and religion.
    Throughout history money and religion were closely linked, for there was little distinction between government and religion.

Exercise 36.3
Sentence combining: Comma splices and fused sentences, p. 97

1   The exact origin of paper money is unknown because it has not survived as coins, shells, and other durable objects have.

Exercise 36.4
Revising: Comma splices and fused sentences, p. 98

What many call the first genocide of modern times occurred during World War I, when the Armenians were deported from their homes in Anatolia, Turkey.

Exercise 37.1
Revising: Mixed sentences, p. 99

1 A hurricane occurs when the winds in a tropical depression rotate counterclockwise at more than seventy-four miles per hour.
2 People fear hurricanes because they can destroy lives and property. [Sentence correct.]

Exercise 37.2
Revising: Repeated subjects and other parts, p. 101

1 Archaeologists and other scientists can often determine the age of their discoveries by means of radiocarbon dating.

Exercise 38.1
Revising: Periods, p. 102

1 The instructor asked when Plato wrote *The Republic*.

Exercise 38.2
Revising: Question marks, p. 102

1 In Homer's *Odyssey*, Odysseus took seven years to travel from Troy to Ithaca. Or was it eight years? Or more?

Exercise 38.3
Revising: Exclamation points, p. 103

1 As the firefighters moved their equipment into place, the police shouted, "Move back!"

Exercise 38.4
Revising: End punctuation, p. 104

When visitors first arrive in Hawaii, they often encounter an unexpected language barrier. Standard English is the language of business and government, but many of the people speak Pidgin English.

Exercise 39.1
Revising: Comma with linked main clauses, p. 105

1 Parents once automatically gave their children the father's last name, but some no longer do.

Exercise 39.2
Sentence combining: Linked main clauses, p. 105

1 The arguments for bestowing the mother's surname on children are often strong and convincing, but they are not universally accepted.

Exercise 39.3
Revising: Comma with introductory elements, p. 107

1 Veering sharply to the right, a large flock of birds neatly avoids a high wall.

2 Moving in a fluid mass is typical of flocks of birds and schools of fish. [Sentence correct.]

Exercise 39.4
Sentence combining: Introductory elements, p. 108

1 In an effort to explain the mysteries of flocks and schools, scientists have proposed bizarre magnetic fields and telepathy.

Exercise 39.5
Revising: Punctuation of nonessential and essential elements, p. 109

1 Anesthesia, which is commonly used during medical operations, once made patients uncomfortable and had serious risks.

2 But new drugs and procedures that have been developed in recent years allow patients under anesthesia to be comfortable and much safer.

Exercise 39.6
Revising: Punctuation of nonessential and essential elements, p. 110

1 Italians insist that Marco Polo, the thirteenth-century explorer, did not import pasta from China.

2 Pasta, which consists of flour and water and often egg, existed in Italy long before Marco Polo left for his travels.

Exercise 39.7
Sentence combining: Essential and nonessential elements, p. 111

1 American colonists first imported pasta from the English, who had discovered it as tourists in Italy.

Exercise 39.8
Revising: Commas with series items, p. 113

1 Photographers who take pictures of flowers need to pay special attention to lighting, composition, and focal point.

Exercise 39.9
Revising: Commas with adjectives, p. 114

1 Most people have seen a blind person being aided by a patient, observant guide dog.

Exercise 39.10
Revising: Punctuation of series and adjectives, p. 115

1   Shoes with high heels were originally designed to protect the wearer's feet from mud, garbage, and animal waste in the streets.

2   The first high heels worn strictly for fashion, however, appeared in the sixteenth century. [Sentence correct.]

Exercise 39.11
Revising: Punctuation of dates, addresses, place names, numbers, p. 116

1   The festival will hold a benefit dinner and performance on March 10, 2007, in Asheville.

Exercise 39.12
Revising: Punctuation of quotations, p. 117

1   The writer and writing teacher Peter Elbow proposes an "open-ended writing process" that "can change you, not just your words." [Sentence correct.]

Exercise 39.13
Revising: Needless and misused commas, p. 117

1   One of the largest aquifers in North America, the Ogallala aquifer, is named after the Ogallala Indian tribe, which once lived in the region and hunted buffalo there. [Sentence correct.]

2   The Ogallala aquifer underlies a region from western Texas through northern Nebraska and has a huge capacity of fresh water that is contained in a layer of sand and gravel.

Exercise 39.14
Revising: Commas, p. 119

1   Ellis Island, New York, reopened for business in 1990, but now the customers are tourists, not immigrants.

2 This spot, which lies in New York Harbor, was the first American soil seen or touched by many of the nation's immigrants.

3 Though other places also served as ports of entry for foreigners, none has the symbolic power of Ellis Island.

Exercise 40.1
Revising: Punctuation between main clauses, p. 121

1 More and more musicians are playing computerized instruments; more and more listeners are worrying about the future of acoustic instruments.

Exercise 40.2
Revising: Punctuation between main clauses with conjunctive adverbs or transitional expressions, p. 121

1 Music is a form of communication like language; the basic elements, however, are not letters but notes.

Exercise 40.3
Sentence combining: Related main clauses, p. 122

1 Electronic instruments are prevalent in jazz and rock music; however, they are less common in classical music.

Exercise 40.4
Revising: Punctuation of main clauses and series items containing commas, p. 124

1 The Indian subcontinent is separated from the rest of the world by clear barriers: the Bay of Bengal and the Arabian Sea to the east and west, respectively; the Indian Ocean to the south; and 1600 miles of mountain ranges to the north.

Exercise 40.5
Revising: Semicolons, p. 124

1 The set, sounds, and actors in the movie captured the essence of horror films. [Sentence correct.]

2 The set was ideal: dark, deserted street; trees dipping their branches over the sidewalks; mist hugging the ground and creeping up the trees; looming shadows of unlighted, turreted houses.

Exercise 41.1
Revising: Colons, p. 125

1 In remote areas of many developing countries, simple signs mark human habitation: a dirt path, a few huts, smoke from a campfire.

Exercise 41.2
Revising: Colons and semicolons, p. 126

1 Sunlight is made up of three kinds of radiation: visible rays; infrared rays, which we cannot see; and ultraviolet rays, which are also invisible. [Sentence correct.]
2 Infrared rays are the longest, measuring 700 nanometers and longer, while ultraviolet rays are the shortest, measuring 400 nanometers and shorter.

Exercise 42.1
Forming possessives, p. 128

1 In the myths of ancient Greeks, the goddesses' roles vary widely.
2 Demeter's responsibility is the fruitfulness of the earth.

Exercise 42.2
Revising: Apostrophes with possessives, p. 129

1 The eastern coast of Belize was once a fisherman's paradise, but overfishing caused the fishing industry's sharp decline in this Central American country.

Exercise 42.3
Distinguishing between plurals and possessives, p. 130

1 Demeter may be the oldest of the ancient Greek gods, older than Zeus.

Exercise 42.4
Revising: Misuses of the apostrophe, p. 131

1 Research is proving that <u>athletes</u> who excel at distance running have physical characteristics that make them faster than most people.

Exercise 42.5
Revising: Contractions and personal pronouns, p. 132

1 Roald Dahl's children's novel *James and the Giant Peach* has been enjoyed by each generation of readers since its first publication in 1961. [Sentence correct.]
2 <u>It's</u> a magical story of adventure and friendship.

Exercise 42.6
Forming contractions, p. 132

1 <u>She'd</u> rather be dancing.

Exercise 42.7
Revising: Contractions and personal pronouns, p. 134

1 In Greek myth the goddess Demeter has a special fondness for Eleusis, near Athens, and <u>its</u> people.

Exercise 42.8
Revising: Apostrophes, p. 135

1 Landlocked Chad is among the <u>world's</u> most troubled countries.
2 The <u>peoples</u> of Chad are poor: <u>their</u> average per capita income equals $1000 a year.

Exercise 43.1
Revising: Double and single quotation marks, p. 136

1 <u>"Why,"</u> the lecturer asked, <u>"do we say 'Bless you!' or something else when people sneeze but not acknowledge coughs, hiccups, and other eruptions?"</u>

Exercise 43.2
Revising: Quotation marks for titles, p. 136

1   In Chapter 8, titled "How to Be Interesting," the author ex-
    plains the art of conversation.

Exercise 43.3
Revising: Quotation marks, p. 137

1   In the title essay of her book "The Death of the Moth" and
    Other Essays, Virginia Woolf describes the last moments of a
    "frail and diminutive body." [Underlining correct for book
    title, but essay title within it is quoted.]

Exercise 43.4
Revising: Quotation marks, p. 138

1   In one class we talked about a passage from "I Have a Dream,"
    the speech delivered by Martin Luther King, Jr., on the steps
    of the Lincoln Memorial on August 28, 1963:

Exercise 44.1
Revising: Dashes, p. 139

1   The movie-theater business is undergoing dramatic changes—
    changes that may affect what movies are made and shown.

Exercise 44.2
Revising: Parentheses, p. 140

1   Many of those involved in the movie business agree that multi-
    screen complexes are good for two reasons: (1) they cut the costs
    of exhibitors, and (2) they offer more choices to audiences.

Exercise 44.3
Using ellipsis marks, p. 141

1   "To be able to read the Bible in the vernacular was a liberating experience._ . . ._"

Exercise 44.4
Revising: Dashes, parentheses, ellipsis marks, brackets, slashes, p. 142

1   "Let all the learned say what they can, _/_ 'Tis ready money makes the man."

2   These two lines of poetry by the Englishman William Somerville (1645–1742) may apply to a current American economic problem.

Exercise 45.1
Distinguishing between ie and ei, p. 144

1   brief
2   deceive

Exercise 45.2
Revising: ie and ei, p. 144

1   Many people perceive donating blood as a rewarding experience. [Sentence correct.]

2   Giving blood is neither painful nor weird, although many people believe it is both.

Exercise 45.3
Keeping or dropping a final e, p. 145

1   malicious
2   lovable _or_ loveable

Exercise 45.4
Revising: Final e, p. 146

1 For decades scientists have been <u>securing</u> metal and plastic bands to the flippers of penguins and <u>using</u> the numbered bands to observe the birds' behavior.

Exercise 45.5
Keeping or dropping a final y, p. 147

1 implies
2 messier

Exercise 45.6
Revising: Final y, p. 147

1 My neighbor, Mr. Sorsky, often says he is <u>worried</u> about his job.

Exercise 45.7
Doubling consonants, p. 148

1 repairing
2 admittance

Exercise 45.8
Revising: Consonants, p. 149

1 People have always been <u>charmed</u> by the idea of walking on water.

Exercise 45.9
Attaching prefixes, p. 150

1 misplace
2 self-conscious

Exercise 45.10
Revising: Prefixes, p. 151

1 People often seem to regard bacteria as somehow <u>unnatural</u> intruders in human biology.

Exercise 45.11
Forming plurals, p. 151

1 piles
2 donkeys

Exercise 45.12
Revising: Plurals, p. 153

1 Fewer original video games are available these <u>days</u>, but sales and production of <u>sequels</u> to popular games are strong.

Exercise 45.13
Using correct spellings, p. 153

1 Science <u>affects</u> many <u>important</u> aspects of our lives, though many people have a <u>poor</u> understanding of the <u>role</u> of scientific breakthroughs in <u>their</u> health.

Exercise 45.14
Working with a spelling checker, p. 155

1 The <u>weather</u> <u>affects</u> all of us, though <u>its</u> <u>effects</u> are different for different people.

Exercise 45.15
Using hyphens in compound words, p. 155

1 reimburse [correct]
2 de-escalate

Exercise 45.16
Revising: Hyphens, p. 157

1 The African elephant is well known for its size. [Sentence correct.]
2 A male elephant weighs five-and-one-half to six tons, and a female weighs up to four tons.

Exercise 46.1
Revising: Capitals, p. 157

1 San Antonio, Texas, is a thriving city in the Southwest that has always offered much to tourists interested in the roots of Spanish settlement in the New World.
2 Most visitors stop at the Alamo, one of five Catholic missions built by priests to convert Native Americans and to maintain Spain's claims in the area.

Exercise 47.1
Revising: Underlining or italics, p. 159

1 A number of veterans of the war in Vietnam have become prominent writers. [Sentence correct.]
2 Oliver Stone is perhaps the most famous for writing and directing the films Platoon and Born on the Fourth of July.

Exercise 48.1
Revising: Abbreviations, p. 160

1 In an issue of Science magazine, Dr. Virgil L. Sharpton discusses a theory that could help explain the extinction of dinosaurs. [Sentence correct.]
2 According to the theory, a comet or asteroid crashed into the earth about 65 million years ago.

Exercise 49.1
Revising: Numbers, p. 161

1   The planet Saturn is <u>900</u> million miles, or nearly <u>1.5 billion</u> kilometers, from the sun.

Exercise 52.1
Synthesizing sources, p. 163

The key similarities and differences are these:

Similarities: Nadelmann and Posey agree that crackdowns or penalties do not stop the drug trade. Nadelmann and Runkle agree that the drug trade affects the young, who are most impressionable.

Differences: Nadelmann maintains that the illegal drug trade does more to entice youths to drugs than do the drugs themselves, whereas Runkle maintains that the illegality discourages youths from using prohibited drugs. Posey, in contrast to Runkle, claims that penalties do nothing to discourage drug abusers.

Exercise 52.2
Summarizing and paraphrasing, p. 165

Possible summary

Eisinger et al. 44
Federalism, unlike a unitary system, allows the states autonomy. Its strength and its weakness—which are in balance—lie in the regional differences it permits.

Exercise 52.3
Combining summary, paraphrase, and direct quotation, p. 167

Possible answer

Farb 107
Speakers at parties often "unconsciously duel" in conversations in order to assert "dominance" over others.

Exercise 52.4
Introducing and interpreting borrowed material, p. 167

Sample beginning of a paragraph

Why does a woman who is otherwise happy regularly suffer anxiety attacks at the first sign of spring? Why does a man who is otherwise a competent, relaxed driver feel panic whenever he approaches a traffic rotary? According to Willard Gaylin, a professor of psychiatry and a practicing psychoanalyst, such feelings of anxiety are attributable to the uniquely human capacities for remembering, imagining, and forming "symbolic and often unconscious representations" of experiences (23).

Exercise 53.1
Recognizing plagiarism, p. 169

1 Plagiarized: takes phrases directly from the original without quotation marks.

Exercise 58.1
Writing MLA works-cited entries, p. 171

Conte, Christopher. "Networking the Classroom." <u>CQ Researcher</u> 5

(2004): 923-43.